The Midlands

Edited by Allison Dowse

First published in Great Britain in 2005 by:
Young Writers
Remus House
Coltsfoot Drive
Peterborough
PE2 9JX
Telephone: 01733 890066
Website: www.youngwriters.co.uk

SB ISBN 1 84602 107 3

Foreword

Young Writers was established in 1991 and has been passionately devoted to the promotion of reading and writing in children and young adults ever since. The quest continues today. Young Writers remains as committed to the fostering of burgeoning poetic and literary talent as ever.

This year's Young Writers competition has proven as vibrant and dynamic as ever and we are delighted to present a showcase of the best poetry from across the UK. Each poem has been carefully selected from a wealth of *Playground Poets* entries before ultimately being published in this, our thirteenth primary school poetry series.

Once again, we have been supremely impressed by the overall high quality of the entries we have received. The imagination, energy and creativity which has gone into each young writer's entry made choosing the best poems a challenging and often difficult but ultimately hugely rewarding task - the general high standard of the work submitted amply vindicating this opportunity to bring their poetry to a larger appreciative audience.

We sincerely hope you are pleased with our final selection and that you will enjoy *Playground Poets The Midlands* for many years to come.

Contents

The Poems

Dreams And Hopes

D reams are hopes
R easons to be happy
E ating delicious yummy food
A world without war
M y dream is that I have a kitten or a bunny.

H oping there will be peace on Earth
O pen the door of peace
P eace is love
E xcitement in my life
S ee the world.

Aniqa Jhangir (9)

A Poem About My Family

My mum's picking flowers in the garden,
Dad is washing the car,
My brother is playing football and kicked it really high,
My baby brother is clapping his hands,
My grandma is reading a book,
My sister is painting really nicely
And I'm just writing poems that I like.

Athiya Ejaz

My Little Brother

Some people have a sibling of one or the other,
Me, myself, have a baby brother.

He reminds me of Gollum looking for the ring,
But in fact he is not looking for anything.

He is very small with lovely big eyes
And I love him very much which is no surprise.

Melissa Canning (9)
Acocks Green Primary School, Acocks Green

Things I Like

I like reading and writing stories and poems,
I like singing and dancing and watching TV,
It's just a few things I thought you'd like to know about me.

I like chocolate and ice cream and chips from the chip shop,
It's just a few things I like quite a lot.

I like drawing and colouring and I still like the colour pink
But sometimes you know, I just like to sit and think.

I like pop music, lipgloss and all things to do with hair,
I used to like Busted but now I couldn't care.

Of course I like my mum and dad and even my sister sometimes too,
Is there anything you'd like me to know about you?

I'm only eight and I like a lot of things,
Sometimes I wonder what the rest of my life will bring.

Chloe Murphy (8)
Acocks Green Primary School, Acocks Green

Summer Holiday - Acrostic

S ummer is a season everyone enjoys.
U p right in the sky the sun is shining.
M aking lovely pictures to do with summer.
M um and Dad taking me to the park to play.
E veryone likes summer holidays, even parents.
R unning to the beach to have fun.

H olidays are for resting, that's what parents say.
O pen your drink it's too hot.
L ong day we all have a rest.
I t's too hot, everyone goes swimming.
D ays passed by before you know it.
A ll that fun makes you a bit tired.
Y ou and your friends have fun together.
S wimming is a pleasure to end your summer holiday.

Kharam Kaur (10)
Acocks Green Primary School, Acocks Green

Winter Wonderland

Winter snow glistening on the sunlit grass,
Humans made of snow motionless,
Watching all that passes by,
In this winter wonderland.

Rolling snow throughout the park,
More of us are created,
We watch as the days pass by,
In this winter wonderland.

Sun breaks through the cloudy skies,
All my friends slowly melt
And all is left is winter dew,
In this winter wonderland.

Slowly I myself start melting,
Soon I will be no more
Than a puddle on the floor,
No more a winter wonderland.

Deanna Vigers (8)
Acocks Green Primary School, Acocks Green

Inspiration

Inspiration is an action of power that can influence you
And change your life forever.

Inspiration is a message that has been spread.

Inspiration is hearing the pastor preach on Sunday morning.

Inspiration is Jesus dying on the cross to forgive my sins.

Inspiration is Aretha Franklin proving that black people
Can do anything with God behind them.

Inspiration is God, my creator.

Inspiration challenges me to do better,
For no one can take my dignity and self-respect away.

Vanessa May Jones (10)
Acocks Green Primary School, Acocks Green

My Family

My nan and grandad have helped me through dark days,
When I am ill there are no ways
They will comfort me with love and care
And are always there to share.

My dad and sisters are always there,
Even when I don't care,
I really need my sisters there
And my dad gives me love and care.

I love my family the way they are,
I would never swap them with a millionaire,
We all need a family round us,
Even in the most terrible days.

So give your brothers
And sisters a break
Because everyone needs
A family!

Ryan Adkins (10)
Acocks Green Primary School, Acocks Green

My House Move

We are moving today, hooray!
A big garden at our new house, plenty of places to play.
I have my own room, small it may be
But the space in it is only for me.
We are moving today, hooray!
No more brothers in the way,
More space, more room to run around,
No more brothers in my ground.
We are moving today, hooray!
Nice neighbours and I am allowed my friends to stay,
Mum and Dad are happy and no longer snappy,
We are moving today, hooray!

Max Lowry (10)
Acocks Green Primary School, Acocks Green

The Dolphin

Splish, splash in the sea
The dolphin swims with happiness and glee.

Paddling in the ripples, gliding through the waves
Searching for some fish to eat, she has to be brave.

A school of fish swim by
And look her in the eye.

This could be her big chance . . .
Oh no! She missed them!

She has to look for more fish
But cannot find any more.

Oh look! She's found a shipwreck
She starts to explore.

She's found a new place to live
She touches it with her fin.

She will catch fish so easily
That's the life of the dolphin.

Hannah Marie Corrigan (9)
Acocks Green Primary School, Acocks Green

The Victorians

For the Victorians life was bad,
For the Victorians life was sad.
During the day you'd work not play,
During the night you'd have nothing to say.

Life at school was very hard,
They were never off-guard.
When you were cheeky or did something wrong,
I'll tell you now you'd never look strong.

When you came home there would be nothing to eat,
You'd have to wait for Mom to cook tea.

Abbey Jarvis (11)
Acocks Green Primary School, Acocks Green

Seasons

Spring is when flowers grow,
Roses and daisies all in a row,
The spring breeze just passes by,
Maybe the butterflies wonder why.

Summer is full of fun,
Relaxing in the sun,
Summertime will never end,
Autumn is just round the bend.

Autumn is almost here,
Winter is very near,
Farmers cut their corn,
People forget to cut their lawn.

Winter soon comes along,
Birds still sing their song,
Snow falls to the ground,
Covering all around.

Deanna Kitts (10)
Acocks Green Primary School, Acocks Green

Foot

Now you're in the playground you can have some fun,
Let's play a game and start to run,
We could play tig or even hide-and-seek,
I like playtime I've been saying it all week,
I'm moving and grooving and the bell just rings,
When I could have done so many things,
Now I've got to wait for the next day,
So I can go out and then just play,
Then I'll be happy,
'Cause I'm a cheeky chappy!

Jagtar Singh (10)
Acocks Green Primary School, Acocks Green

The Seasons

Spring, summer, autumn, winter,
The seasons come and go.
First it's warm, then it's hot,
Then the crunchy leaves drop off the trees
And then comes the icy snow.

Spring is when blossom comes out
And baby animals are all about,
The leaves on trees turn lush green
And flowers you have never seen.

Summer is when you see the sun
And longer days have begun,
The scorching sun tans us brown
Until the sun has gone down.

Autumn is when you see multicoloured leaves fluttering by
And it goes all misty in the sky.
The branches on trees are now nude
And children bring in harvest food.

Winter is when you see the snow
And everyone's coats start to glow.
People start to wrap up warm
And ice is growing on the lawn.

Spring, summer, autumn, winter,
The seasons come and go.
First it's warm, then it's hot,
The crunchy leaves drop off the trees
And then comes the icy snow.

Nisha Patel (11)
Acocks Green Primary School, Acocks Green

Things

Nobody likes monsters
because they scare you,
you have to watch out
for when they go *'Boo!'*

I like football
because it is fun,
but when I played last week
the other team won.

Children like school
because you learn things,
but when it is art
you get to paint kings.

Books are different
like history and rhyme,
non-fiction could tell you
to count up to nine.

I collect crystals,
they are very shiny,
but when I open the box
I need the metal key.

Now the end of my poem
it's not going in the bin,
all I'm going to do
is hand it in.

Max Wells (8)
Acocks Green Primary School, Acocks Green

My Rhyming A - Z Of Foods

Annie Apple is nice and green, will make you grow and be seen
Billy Banana is yellow and cool, will make you grow nice and tall
Collin Carrot plays in the park, will make you see in the dark
Danny Doughnut is no good, throw him away and you'll be good
Elli Egg is always on the run, so never eat it until it's done
Frankie French Fry is full of fat,
Cook them in the oven and that'll be that
Graham Grape is small and round, eat them all without a sound
Harry Hamburger is so bad, he'll make you grow up to be sad
Ian Ice Cream can be good for you, eat too much he'll be bad for you
Jamey Jam is so sweet, but no good for your teeth
Kelly Kiwi is in a skin, but is so good you'll never give in
Laura Lemon is so sharp, too much will be bad for your heart
Mickey Milk is white and creamy, he'll make you strong extremely
Nigel Nuts is very salty, which isn't very healthy
Olli Olive is a pickle, too much will give you a tickle
Polly Pizza is so round and hot, just remember not to eat a lot
Quinn Quiche is full of flavour, but it won't do anything in your favour
Rodger Ravioli is full of colour, you'll want him for your dinner
Sammy Spaghetti is full of fibre, it'll feel good inside ya
Timmy Takeaway is full of grease, too much will make you obese
Ursula Upside Down Cake is full of sugar,
So don't you dare have another
Velma Vegetable is your mate, so have some on your plate
Willy Waffle is full of holes, so don't have any in your bowls
Xmas Pudding is very nice, eat it once a year and you'll be alright
Yasmin Yorkshire goes well with mash, so don't eat them in a dash
Zena Zucchini Bread is very nutty, eat too much and you'll go nutty!

Terri-Ann Sparrow (10)
Acocks Green Primary School, Acocks Green

Walking In The Rain

The lightning is sharp
Like a Swiss army knife,
It comes down slowly,
You can save your life.

Bright lights of lightning
Coming from clouds,
Here comes the rain
Hitting the crowd.

Bright lights of thunder
Coming from the sky,
Here comes the hail
Seeing the birds fly.

Ryan Wright (10)
Alcott Hall J&I School, Chelmsley Wood

Cold

Monotonous clouds cover the sky,
The sky has turned completely black,
I let out an enormous sigh,
I bet that nobody is in the park,
It's damp outside, it's gloomy within.

I'm very sad I can't manage a grin,
I can't even be bothered to play,
The wind is howling right by my side,
There's nothing to do, there's nothing to say,
It's cold outside, inside me it's chilly.

Annie-Mai Goode (9)
Alcott Hall J&I School, Chelmsley Wood

Disaster!

Thunder is roaring,
Run away dears,
My dad is snoring,
Cover your ears!

There is now a storm,
Snowflakes falling.
I would love to be warm,
It's appalling.

Raindrops reach the ground,
There is now a flood
Surrounding the town,
Leaving wet mud.

Fern Burnett (9)
Alcott Hall J&I School, Chelmsley Wood

Gloomy

The lights are all on though it's just nearly 11am,
The sky is all dull,
No blue in the sky,
The world is all lifeless, no reason to live,
It's gloomy outside, it's cheerless to live.

There's nothing to do inside these walls,
Too freezing to play outside,
It's a miserable day and all last week,
It's too freezing inside, the boiler's broken down,
It's dull outside, inside me it's lifeless.

Shawn Taylor (9)
Alcott Hall J&I School, Chelmsley Wood

Weather

The lightning is sharp
Like a Swiss army knife,
It comes down so quickly
And could cost you your life.

The rain is so heavy
On a stormy night,
With crashes of thunder
It could give you a fright.

The hail is hard,
It is just like small stones,
It hits you all over
And maybe breaks bones.

Ryan Morris (10)
Alcott Hall J&I School, Chelmsley Wood

Rainstorm

I'm walking my dog,
Rain's coming down,
I'm getting so wet,
Without a sound.

The drains have flooded,
The lightning's flashed,
I nearly got struck,
Storm clouds have crashed.

The lightning has stopped,
Can't hear a sound,
Look out, here comes the sun,
I'm on the ground.

Amber Sullivan (10)
Alcott Hall J&I School, Chelmsley Wood

Weather

Bright clips of lightning
Down from the sky,
No one has seen it
Up very high.

Mixed with the rumbles
Coming from town,
Splashing on houses
Rain is falling down.

Hail is falling,
it just hurt me,
It hurts everyone
As I can see.

Grant Burbidge (9)
Alcott Hall J&I School, Chelmsley Wood

Rainstorm

I'm out with my pals,
Down comes the rain
Splashing in puddles,
It is a pain.

The thunder is here,
The dog is so scared,
My dad is in bed,
My cat sits and stares.

The lightning has come,
Shut all the doors,
It will stop soon enough,
See how it roars.

Ryan Pettifer (10)
Alcott Hall J&I School, Chelmsley Wood

Rain Poem

On a rainy night when things are a fright,
A nasty storm clashes, rains falls in the night.
A dark rainy cloud, is grey all around,
A child screams in fright and wakes up all the night.

Splitter, splatter on the doors, wetness falls and lightning roars,
Drainpipes are starting to flood, everywhere around the hood.
The storm does not inspire and sets the trees on fire,
Your shoes will get dirty because of the wet mud.

Thunderstorm stewing, people are viewing,
The clouds are dark, dogs start to bark.
Puddles flood around the mud, lightning strikes around the hood,
Lightning is very hard, all it leaves is one red mark.

Jack Paget (10)
Alcott Hall J&I School, Chelmsley Wood

Rain

The rain was hard,
The rain was strong,
It caused thunder
All night long.

I heard the rain fall,
I saw it drop,
It was horrible,
It scared my dog.

The rain and thunder
Was really bad.
I wanted some fun
And I was sad.

Mitchell Atterbury (10)
Alcott Hall J&I School, Chelmsley Wood

Raindrops

Raindrops falling
From the sky so high.
Raindrops tapping,
They fall from the sky.

Thunder shocking
Like an army knife.
Lightning rocking,
It could cost your life.

Lightning shooting
In-between we run.
Shooting lightning
Blinds us like the sun.

Alex Baker (10)
Alcott Hall J&I School, Chelmsley Wood

Rain Poem

I'm out with my friends,
Without a sound
I am very wet,
I'm running round.

I heard the door knock,
Rain on the grass,
I saw the rain fall,
Will the storm pass?

The rain is stopping,
The sun is out,
Look there's a rainbow.

Shanice Taylor
Alcott Hall J&I School, Chelmsley Wood

When The Rain Comes Down

When the rain comes down
It looks so pretty.
When the thunder roars
It's almost witty.

Thunder and lightning
Are exciting,
They're so frightening,
I hate lightning.

I hope it stops raining,
Oh why, oh why,
Why's it not draining?

Sophie Bottrell (10)
Alcott Hall J&I School, Chelmsley Wood

One Day Out

I'm out with my friends,
Here comes the rain,
It is getting wet,
Even the drain.

Thunder is coming,
Not very good,
It's making noises,
Now there's a flood.

Now it is lightning,
What shall I do?
I am soaking wet,
I've lost my shoe.

Tara Smith (10)
Alcott Hall J&I School, Chelmsley Wood

The Sun

There's the sun hip hip hooray,
Now we can go out to play.
We don't need a coat,
Or a big blue boat
Because we can have fun
And eat a buttered bun.
We can have water fights
And fly our dragon kites.
We can have a nibble
So don't cry and dribble.
We can eat an ice lolly
And let out the parrot Polly.
Let's go to the beach,
There's no time to teach.
Put on your sunglasses
And I'll get the airport passes
Because there's the big burning sun.

Curtis Talbot (10)
Alcott Hall J&I School, Chelmsley Wood

I Don't Want To Go!

I watch the little white icicles fall with grace,
They fall all over the place.
They come from out of the sky,
If you stand at the window you can watch them go by.
I put on my hat and gloves so I can play,
I would not put them on any other day.
Your mom calls you in but you do not want to go,
You hate to stop playing in the beautiful white snow.

Measha Thomas (10)
Alcott Hall J&I School, Chelmsley Wood

Hooray

Hip hip hooray, let's go and play
When the girls and boys go in the hay.

Ice cream dripping so tender and cool,
People swimming so far and small,
Seagulls talking so loud and quick.

Sun is beaming so far away,
Sunglasses on, deckchairs out,
What a wonderful day it is.

Danielle Lee (11)
Alcott Hall J&I School, Chelmsley Wood

The Snow

The snow is falling in the air,
Different shapes and sizes everywhere.
Snowflakes falling on my head,
Wish I could just lie in my bed.
It's very cold all around,
Especially on the ground.

Kieran Barter (10)
Alcott Hall J&I School, Chelmsley Wood

It's Sunny

It's sunny outside on the beach,
I sit and watch the waves come in
While I eat my lovely ice cream,
It feels cold dripping down my hand
And my feet are in the boiling hot sand.
I feel the slimy seaweed trickle away over my feet,
Then I go back to rest.

Rhianne Ikin (10)
Alcott Hall J&I School, Chelmsley Wood

A Summer Sun

I go to the beach every year
And sit on my deckchair.
I lick my flavoured ice cream
As my sister started to scream.

Because she is scared of the sea
She came and ran to me,
As I put my bikini on
And swam in the sea with my mom.

Kayleigh Restell (10)
Alcott Hall J&I School, Chelmsley Wood

The Sun

The sun is out, hip hip hooray,
There are people on sunbeds
And children playing games today.
Adults buying drinks all around,
There isn't a frown in sight
Until that time of day
That time of day called night.

Scott Kiely (10)
Alcott Hall J&I School, Chelmsley Wood

Sun

The sun is out shining away,
We're all on the beach, it is a great day.
Surfers on the waves coming closer to shore,
Children are playing away.
It is a great holiday,
We're away from school, hip hip hooray.

Joshua Bromage (10)
Alcott Hall J&I School, Chelmsley Wood

A Day At The Beach

In the summer it's very hot,
The sun is shining in every spot.
I go to the beach every day,
On the sand I go and play.
Building sandcastles with my spade,
Then I nap in the shade.
After that I swim in the sea,
But then my mom says to me,
'Look there's the ice cream van.'
So then I go and ask the man,
What's the best ice cream
You have in your machine?
Then I have a nice ice cone,
Then it's time for me to go home.

Lauren Timmins (11)
Alcott Hall J&I School, Chelmsley Wood

Floating Wool

Walking round and round
Without a sound
I see floating wool,
It's getting closer and closer,
It will put us in water
Then it starts to tip water out
But we are where about.

Thick black wool ever so low,
Can you see it moving really slow?
The heavier it gets
The more it lets out,
Are you ready, here it comes,
Umbrellas go up and wellies go on.

Stephanie Simpson (11)
Alcott Hall J&I School, Chelmsley Wood

The Sun

Here's the sun, thank God for that,
Winter is over so have fun,
Hang up your coat, gloves and hat,
Bring out the sunglasses
And bring out your sports bottle,
Bring out your red boat
And take it to the lake,
No need for cars because you can walk,
So hang up the car keys
And bring out the sandals,
My mom's sunbathing,
My sisters are having fun in the pool,
My dad is watering the plants
And I'm having a water fight.

Joshua Arnold (11)
Alcott Hall J&I School, Chelmsley Wood

Fog

This is black and scary,
It looks very hairy,
It's a horrible smoke,
As dark as Coke,
It's impossible to see through,
It will be the same to you too.

Could there be a monster?
The floor is like a lobster,
Don't know where to go,
Even Santa can't see, ho, ho, ho,
This is everywhere,
This will give you quite a scare,
If you stay out of it you'll become aware.

Ashley Blewitt (10)
Alcott Hall J&I School, Chelmsley Wood

The Tsunami

Those people in Asia,
All so poor,
Spare a thought
For all those there.

How sad it is
To see them die,
People in the world
Give them some aid.

We are so lucky
But they are not,
The people in Asia
So scared and alone.

On December 26th
This horrific thing happened
Right after Christmas
In 2004.

Philip Winnall (10)
Alcott Hall J&I School, Chelmsley Wood

Snowflake

Snowflakes falling all around,
Here and there and touch the ground.
Cold snowflakes falling on my head,
Wish I was in my lovely warm bed.
My friends are playing on their sledge,
Slips and slides and in the hedge!

Build a snowman in the snow,
The snow's already melting, oh no.
I put on my hat and gloves to play,
We're having a snowball fight hip hip hooray!

Sally Perks (11)
Alcott Hall J&I School, Chelmsley Wood

The Sun

The sun is ever so bright,
Don't look at it, it's not right,
Everyone is playing in the sun,
Everybody is having fun.

Now the sun is going down,
Everyone is coming back from town,
All children are sad, there is no more sun,
But tomorrow they'll have so much fun.

Omar Harb (10)
Alcott Hall J&I School, Chelmsley Wood

The Lightning

The lightning has come out to scare you and me,
To scare us from above,
To scare us with its roar
When the clouds go black
And the sky goes grey.

The lightning is no nice thing today,
When lightning strikes us from above
With its colours and their terrible stuff.

Alex Porter (10)
Alcott Hall J&I School, Chelmsley Wood

Snow Falling

Snow falling so fast,
Me and my friends playing in the snow
Wearing my gloves, scarf and hat.
Going down a steep hill on my sledge,
Got to remember there might be ice.
Whoops! told you there might be ice.
Now I have got to go in and have my dinner
And stay in because it's so cold.

Cheyenne Conway (11)
Alcott Hall J&I School, Chelmsley Wood

Sly Red Fox

Sly red fox creeps through the dark,
Stops to listen, hears a bark.
Sneaks off down to find its prey,
Sleeps down its hole for the rest of the day.

Comes out of his hole, pricks up his ears,
Struts along without any fears.
Out comes the farmer with his gun,
Now it's time to run, run, run.

Being a fox is a dangerous life,
Full of enemies and strife.
He just tries to feed his young,
But people hate him all day long.

Tom Young (10)
All Saints CE (C) Primary School, Rangemore

The Cat

The cat with sharp senses
Always jumping over fences.
His eyes are like beaming lights,
Not afraid of any heights.

He always scratches
And leaves you with many patches,
But before the day starts
He is off again on one of those carts.

But then before the day ends
He is back again
With no friends.

Callum McBride (11)
All Saints CE (C) Primary School, Rangemore

Tigers

Tigers are wild,
Some are very mild,
Some are just playful,
Just like a child.

Some are noisy,
Some are clumsy,
Some are crazy,
But some are lazy.

Some are nosy,
Some are dozy,
Most are dangerous,
But not so cosy.

Tigers are big,
Some of them dig.
As they widen up their eyes
Some play tig.

Kimberley Crowe (11)
All Saints CE (C) Primary School, Rangemore

School

School is like the seasons,
It's changing all the time,
You do not need a reason
To go to school and shine.

Although we do work hard,
We have some time to play,
At 3.15 we all run out, jump and shout hooray,
We've finished our work from all of the day.

Paris Turner (11)
All Saints CE (C) Primary School, Rangemore

Dogs

I love dogs and so do you,
Even though they wee and poo,
In the kennel they sleep all day,
Until we come home, then they play.

Labradors, collies, any kind we love,
Great Danes, terriers in the pub,
Golden dogs to black dogs, mongrel to pedigree,
When we ask them a question they always agree.

Pedigree to Winalot,
To Baker's Complete,
From puppy to senior
Then enjoy what they eat.

They do their training,
Sit, down, stand,
But most of all,
They like the treats from my hand.

That is the joy of having a dog.

Charlotte Carpenter (10)
All Saints CE (C) Primary School, Rangemore

Dogs!

Dogs always like to bark,
Or like to go for a walk in the park.
They love to play with a toy,
No matter the kind, girl or boy.
Having fun, they run and run,
When they come home they lie in a heap,
Then night comes, they fall asleep.

Natasha Woolley (10)
All Saints CE (C) Primary School, Rangemore

Clouds

I watch the clouds go by,
And I wonder why,
They're like cotton wool,
Even though the sky's so dull.

Why are they so fluffy?
In the sky so puffy,
They stay still all the time,
Even when the sun will shine.

When I walk around
The clouds look very round,
They drift around the sun
Having lots of fun.

Harriet Hughes (11)
All Saints CE (C) Primary School, Rangemore

The Shed Monster

There's a monster in our garden shed,
I've seen it - it's covered in spikes,
About the sea of spiderwebs,
It just ate the old bikes.

When it was time to mow the lawn
Dad opened the shed door,
And out it came (the mower was torn),
But fell through a hole in the floor.

We crowded round to have a look,
It was a prickly ball,
We looked for the creature in a book,
A hedgehog had taken the fall!

Alice Cockeram (9)
All Saints CE (C) Primary School, Rangemore

My Dog Slayed A Dragon

My dog slayed a dragon
Using karate and kung fu.
My dog slayed a dragon
Doing what doggies do.

My dog slayed a dragon
Using no chain mail or armour.
My dog slayed a dragon
And practised on a farmer.

When my dog slayed the dragon
He used his claws and raged.
When my dog slayed the dragon
He never even got praised.

Sam Peach (9)
All Saints CE (C) Primary School, Rangemore

Dear Water

Dear water,
Just a quick note,
Thanks for keeping me afloat,
Very safe on my boat,
As I wear my lucky coat.

Thank you for sending fish here,
I enjoy them with my beer.
As I frown
You'll never let me down.

As you come every day
I think of you in a special way.
I like when you're calm and still,
From your pal, Fisherman Bill.

Louis Ranyard (9)
All Saints CE (C) Primary School, Rangemore

My Pets

I have a quail
Who I want to swim with a whale.
I have a horse,
He can jump of course.
I have a fish,
He helps me make a wish.
I have a dog,
She's a bit of a hog.
I have a pup,
She drinks from a cup.
I have some sheep,
My mum feels like Little Bo-Peep.

Christopher Eaton (10)
All Saints CE (C) Primary School, Rangemore

The Funky Monkey

There was a little monkey
Who was very funky,
He danced all day,
He danced all night
And never wanted to fight.

But then his mum said to him,
'It's time to get chunky.'
'But Mum I want to dance, not
Fight some chunky monkey!'

So then monkey packed his bags,
Fed up of all his mum's nags.
'Bye Mum, see you soon,
Might come back as a big baboon!'

Francesca Harper (10)
All Saints CE (C) Primary School, Rangemore

White

He got his fur from the snow
And the stripes he has are coal.
His teeth he has are as sharp as ice
And burn like boiling water.
He got his ears from the bat
And claws from the purring cat.

The tiger is cute and looks like a stray,
But if you go near he'll take you away.

Chloe Kersey (10)
All Saints CE (C) Primary School, Rangemore

Jaguar And Sloth

J aguar prowls silently and secretly,
A lways protecting its cubs.
G ently sneaking towards its prey,
U nseen it creeps through the night.
A lways out hunting for food
R eturning to its cubs at last.

A nother new day, lots of rain,
N ight falls, the noise begins,
D eep in the jungle you will find the 'man in a mask'.

S loths are as slow as can be,
L ong sharp claws.
O nly goes to the toilet once a week.
T wisting round the branches,
H anging from the trees.

Esme Dudley (9)
Bournebrook CE Primary School, Fillongley

Rainforest Cake Recipe

A coil of deadly anaconda,
12 litres of water (rain and water),
10 spoonfuls of leaves,
A pinch of mud,
Lots of insects (doesn't matter which kind),
6 tree trunks,
1 big bright flower,
20 metres of branches,
Mix together in a hollow tree,
Bake the mixture in the sun for 1 hour,
Once you have baked it decorate it with mud,
Twigs, leaves, flowers
And a sprinkling of animals.

Chloe Broad (8)
Bournebrook CE Primary School, Fillongley

Rainforests

R ainforests are colourful and bright
A nd shadowy, even though it's not night.
I t's tropical, beautiful and amazing,
N ot always safe, terrifying.
F or if you look at the top of the trees it looks like broccoli.
O range, purple, yellow and green all grows in the canopy.
R eptiles slithering through the leaves.
E agles looking out for their prey.
S ounds like a bus full of monkeys.
T arantulas climbing up the tree,
S o I'd watch out, it's very scary . . .

Nancy Gibson (9)
Bournebrook CE Primary School, Fillongley

The Rainforest

Leaves curling like a cup,
Then bending with the weight of the raindrops.
Vivid coloured tropical flowers,
Monkeys chattering like excited children.
The sleepy sloth hangs lazily from his branch.
Insects busily scamper in-between the roots.
High above the birds swoop and dive.
The rainbow-coloured parrot visits the huge trees.
Trees stretch into the sky like Jack's beanstalk
Disappearing beyond the clouds.
Snakes slithering silently, secretly searching for their supper.
Damp, warm air wraps around you like a cloak.
The harpy eagle begins to hunt.
Tiny little buds growing.
Sunset falls slowly. Jaguars appear.
A beautiful and magical forest!

Emily Metcalf (10)
Bournebrook CE Primary School, Fillongley

Rainforest Poem

R estless animals rest their heads,
A nacondas slither silently over the forest floor,
I nsects grow to be enormous,
N oisy monkeys swing through the trees,
F antastic animals scuffle around for food,
O ver the top of your head monkeys swing,
R eady to pounce on its prey the jaguar waits,
E very animal is different,
S loths hang upside down for ages,
T reetops look like broccoli florets.

Caroline Russell (8)
Bournebrook CE Primary School, Fillongley

The Anaconda

An anaconda slithering
slowly in the undergrowth.
Nasty and deadly
the anaconda eyeing its prey.
Alert and ready
for its next meal.
Constricting the life
out of its victims.
Only the lucky
and brave can survive.
Nothing to fear
so it sleeps when it wants.
Down in the waters
up high in the trees.
Amazon king
the mighty anaconda.

Oliver Parkes (10)
Bournebrook CE Primary School, Fillongley

Rainforest

R ain falling everywhere,
A n anaconda slithering through the undergrowth,
I t is hot and steamy there,
N oisy howler monkeys screaming in the trees,
F ascinating colours everywhere you look,
O ld harpy eagle flying in the sky,
R eptiles rummaging everywhere,
E verything is very loud,
S leepless sloth hanging upside down,
T rees so tall you can't see the tops.

Abby Wilcox (8)
Bournebrook CE Primary School, Fillongley

Howler Monkey

H eights are their speciality
O nly eats fruit and leaves
W inding their tails round the mighty trees
L ong oval faces
E njoying playing in the trees
R ainforests are noisy with monkeys.

M onkeys climb in the tall green trees.
O ver and under the treetops they swing
N estling o' so high
K eeping a watch on their babies
E choing through the forest their howls run out
Y elling in the treetops.

Ella McKeown (9)
Bournebrook CE Primary School, Fillongley

Rainforest

R ainforests are huge and wide,
A mazing plants live there,
I n there are creepy animals,
N ew and old, small and tall,
F rogs are poisonous,
O celot are beautifully patterned,
R eptiles are scampering,
E normous leaves block the way,
S loths are hairy and hang upside down,
T all trees that go up to the sunlight.

Serena Sanghera (9)
Bournebrook CE Primary School, Fillongley

Rainforest Rap

Rainforest animals big and round,
Short or hairy, just listen to the sound.

Howler monkeys loud and clear,
Only just they're filled with fear.

Snakes slither through the leaves,
All around the dark green trees.

Sloths hang up on the branches
Eating all their grub sandwiches.

Butterflies' beautiful wings,
The forest is full of wonderful things.

Georgia Whittle (10)
Bournebrook CE Primary School, Fillongley

Rainforest Dream

R aining, it's raining all over again, pitter-patter,
A naconda, watch out, run away, hiss, hiss,
I t is absolutely steaming hot,
N oisy and loud all day and night,
F rightening and fierce the jaguar prowls,
O n and on the howler monkey squeals,
R aring to go the butterfly's always fluttering,
E normous trees taller than a house,
S loths are the slowest creatures ever,
T oucans searching for food.

Georgia Manning (9)
Bournebrook CE Primary School, Fillongley

A Rainforest Poem

Rainforest animals different sizes,
small and round.
It would deafen you
to hear the sound.

Sloths sleeping high
up in a tree.
If we had a race
he couldn't beat me.

Howler monkeys howling
all through the day.
Started in June,
finished in May.

Harpy eagles gliding
through the air.
If they caught a little mouse
I bet they wouldn't share.

Anacondas heavy
and very, very long,
but not as nice
as a hummingbird's song.

Toucans drinking
coconut milk
and butterflies fly by
with wings of silk.

Jaguars silently hunt
for their prey.
If they could talk
I wonder what they might say.

Rainforest animals different sizes,
small and round.
It would deafen you
to hear the sound.

Taylor Dunn (8)
Bournebrook CE Primary School, Fillongley

Rainforest Poem

S leeps high up in trees all day.
L azily hangs upside down from branches.
E xtraordinary rainforest creature.
E very hour of every day it sleeps.
P rotecting its babies
Y oung sloths cling to their mother's fur.

S lowest creature ever in the world.
L eaves are its usual diet.
O nly eats leaves and drinks water to live.
T here are different kinds of sloth: two-toed and three.
H angs upside down in the tree.

Leah James (8)
Bournebrook CE Primary School, Fillongley

The Rainforest

R ain all the time
A nacondas look for their prey.
I nsects crawl around.
N oisy monkeys screaming all day.
F rightening cheetahs scare you away.
O ld snakes slither slowly.
R iver Amazon flows down the rainforest.
E normous eagles catch prey in their huge feet.
S leepy sloths snooze all day.
T all trees wave in the air.

Stuart Robinson (8)
Bournebrook CE Primary School, Fillongley

Sleepy Sloth

S low I may be, but I'm not stupid.
L ittle insects think I am.
E normous trees that I hang upside down from.
E normous leaves that I eat.
P eople say I look like a monkey with no tail.
Y ou won't see me during the day, only at night.

S ome sloths are my friend, but not all.
L ittle baby sloths are so cute.
O ne kind of sloth is two-toed.
T hree-toed sloth is what I am.
H elp save the rainforest, my home, please.

Annabelle Houston (9)
Bournebrook CE Primary School, Fillongley

Anaconda

A nacondas are smooth and scaly,
N o animal can escape from them,
A nimals are petrified,
C rush their prey,
O ften found in the water,
N ever have eye contact with them,
D imensionally unchallenged,
A mazing anaconda.

Bradley Russell (9)
Bournebrook CE Primary School, Fillongley

A Jaguar Poem

J umping from tree to tree
A jaguar quietly prowls through the undergrowth,
G igantic claws tear its prey,
U sing stealth to creep up on animals,
A gile and fierce,
R unning silently through the rainforest.

Jack Davis (10)
Bournebrook CE Primary School, Fillongley

The Sloth

T he sloth is sleeping
H ungry as can be
E ating leaves from the canopy.

S low as can be
L ong sharp claws
O nly going to the toilet once a week
T wisting round tree
H ow can we find him?

Jade Lawson (10)
Bournebrook CE Primary School, Fillongley

Ice Dragon

My ice dragon has silver shining scales
All over his back.
His wings are magical and shine in the night,
His eyes are glittery,
Like little crystal balls,
His body is covered in icy blue dots,
His body glistens in the night,
His ears flap in the moonlight,
As I feel the silky skin
There are icicles all over.

Emmen Ali (8)
Castlecroft Primary School, Castlecroft

The Ice Dragon

Ice like icicles glittering in the snow,
Sapphire for the wings that shine in the rain,
For his eyes bright ruby crystals,
His back with sparkling emeralds that glisten in the snow,
His belly transparent,
His scales very slippery if you touch them.

Jack Rownes (8)
Castlecroft Primary School, Castlecroft

The Ice Dragon

The gleam of the ice dragon,
Shines in the air like a star.

His icy breath blows out a cool, soft wind
That blows all the hotness away,.

His scaled silky wings,
Zoom in the air like a bird.

His crystal eyes have a sheen
When he flies by.

His mountainous clear body,
Shines like ice.

He flies past the mountains
Leaving shimmering ice patterns.

Anneka Ghafar (9)
Castlecroft Primary School, Castlecroft

The Ice Dragon

The ice dragon's gleaming breath
Feels like the coldest metal.
The ice he breathes out is rough
Like his bumpy wings.
The ice dragon's scales go *clink . . . clink . . . clink*
When his back starts to melt.
His ruby-red eyes look like a twinkling volcano.

I hope I *never* meet this dragon,
That I know has claws as sharp as razors,
And teeth as sharp as swords.

I hope I don't *ever, ever* meet this dragon.

Sharon Tiryaki (9)
Castlecroft Primary School, Castlecroft

The Sea

The sea is a prancing, dancing unicorn,
Flying along the shore,
Kicking its soft gentle hooves
On the hard rocks and smooth pebbles,
Shaking and swishing its long, beautiful tail.
Its mane swirling up like a twister,
Crying out and singing in the moonlight.

It flicks up its swaying tail
While dashing through the air,
This beautiful creature loves dancing,
Jumping and leaping on the shore.
It jumps round and around
And sprays if you go too near,
it rocks like a cradle,
Singing itself to sleep with a lullaby.

Katie Astbury (9)
Castlecroft Primary School, Castlecroft

The Ice Dragon

I love the gleam and silver of the ice dragon,
Its silver scales and wings,
Look at its frozen, icy, mirror breath,
And its ruby dark eyes.
It zooms in the air,
Like a star in the bright blue sky.

It is transparent like glass,
With no dark mysterious shadow.
The ice dragon breathes out ice patterns,
And has sparkly metal scales.
He lives in the mountains of ice and snow.

Ashley Hollingsworth (9)
Castlecroft Primary School, Castlecroft

I Would Like To Paint . . .

I would like to paint
The sea as a white horse
Leaving foam in its path.

I would like to paint
The smoothness of the shells
As a silky blanket.

I would like to paint
The roughness of the sand
As it pushes between my toes.

I would like to paint
The whiteness of the seagulls
As they scoop and dive.

I would like to paint
The stillness of the pebbles
As they shimmer in the sea.

I would like to paint
The movement of the crabs
As they scuttle across the sand.

Amy Deeley (10)
Castlecroft Primary School, Castlecroft

Ice Dragon

I like the sparkling silver of him,
I like the bony scales of him,
I like the black crystal nose of him,
I like the spiky tail of him,
I like the silky wings of him,
I like the big fat belly of him,
I like the clink, clank back of him,
I like the dark ruby eyes of him,
I like the icy breath of him.

Daniel Burgwin (9)
Castlecroft Primary School, Castlecroft

I Would Like To Paint . . .

I would like to paint the seagulls
catching the flapping
of their wings.

I would like to paint the white horses
as they gallop
over the sand.

I would like to paint the rock pools
as the crabs
scuttle for food.

I would like to paint the sand
as it kidnaps
my feet.

I would like to paint the sound of the waves
as they lap against
the shore.

I would like to paint the sound of laughter
and screams
from the pier.

Sharna Khan-Bishton (11)
Castlecroft Primary School, Castlecroft

Things I Like About The Ice Dragon

The glaze and gloss and glitz of her,
The gleam and glow and glisten of her,
The crackle and clink and clonk of her,
The scaly back and freeze of her,
The purpley stars and sheen on her,
The ruby eyes and reflection of her.

Hollie Cottam (8)
Castlecroft Primary School, Castlecroft

I Would Like To Paint . . .

I would like to paint the seagulls,
Hovering over the sea, threaded on the wind.

I would like to paint the pebbles
Rippling in the sea.

I would like to paint the ruined sandcastle,
Demolished by the waves.

I would like to paint the crabs,
Trotting along the sandy seashore.

I would like to paint the shaggy dog,
Jumping enthusiastically in the sea.

I would like to paint the starfish
Washed up on the beach.

I would like to paint the pebbles,
Shining in the sun.

I would like to paint all the people
Having fun.

Sebastian Kinsey (11)
Castlecroft Primary School, Castlecroft

Ice Dragon

The ice dragon breathes out silver twinkling stars,
Silky, purple, icicle crystals, falling from the sparkling sky,
Scales crinkling on the ice, making funny sounds,
Gliding with glitter,
Purple diamonds falling from the stars and moon,
Making beautiful shapes,
Clear icicles like sharp teeth, shining bright,
Dragon wings flapping very light.

Katie Martin (8)
Castlecroft Primary School, Castlecroft

The Ice Dragon

I like the cold breath of him,
I like the blue-green colour of him,
I like the sparkly shine of him,
I like the icicle claws of him,
I like the clanking sound of him,
I like the shiny silky wings of him,
I like the slippery, slidey scales of him,
I like the transparent body of him,
I like the ruby eyes of him,
I like the gold and emerald of him,
I like the smooth cold of him.

Ashley Merrick (9)
Castlecroft Primary School, Castlecroft

Ice Dragon

My ice dragon has ruby and emerald eyes that twinkle,
My ice dragon is made with crystal scales,
My ice dragon breathes silver stars shining in the dark,
My ice dragon has sparkling wings and a golden mirror,
My ice dragon loves to breathe snow-white mist everywhere,
My ice dragon loves me and I love him.

Lauren Tinsley (8)
Castlecroft Primary School, Castlecroft

Ice Dragons

Their cream crystal wings float in the blue sky,
Their ruby-red eyes gleam and glisten in the air,
They slip and slide through the snow,
Their tails swish and swoosh,
Their feet clink and clang as they walk.

Annesah Ghafar (9)
Castlecroft Primary School, Castlecroft

The Sea

The sea is a baby unicorn,
Gently clip-clopping along the smooth pebbles,
With her swaying, flowing mane brushing
The tumbling, shining pebbles.

The rushing unicorn dances
Along the calm sea
With her sparkling hooves,
I can see in my mind
A beautiful, sparkling, snow-white baby unicorn
Dancing along the beach.

In winter when it is all cold
I sometimes go to the beach,
I see my lovely snow-white unicorn,
I let her come home with me sometimes.

When it is spring, she goes back to the beach,
When it rains, she sometimes makes a dent in the sand,
But in summer she goes away.

Chelsea Henry (8)
Castlecroft Primary School, Castlecroft

In A Moment of Silence

In a moment of silence
You can hear a ladybird crawling.

In a moment of silence
You can hear a spider run.

In a moment of silence
You can hear an eyelid flicker.

In a moment of silence
You can hear snow falling.

Adam Tinsley (11)
Castlecroft Primary School, Castlecroft

The Sea

The sea is a dangerous bull,
It charges around splashing
Waves everywhere.
Sometimes the water goes over the cliffs,
He roars, rattling the lighthouses.

He leaps onto ships breaking them down,
He fights the biggest waves in the world,
The bull rattles the moon,
And turns the sea into a torrent.
It sweeps houses away.

But in summer
The bull is peaceful,
People can have a safe journey at sea,
He is the nicest bull in the world
In the summer.

Jon-Marc Vukelic (9)
Castlecroft Primary School, Castlecroft

I Would Like To Paint . . .

I would like to paint
The dolphin jumping in and out of the water
With the sunset lighting it up with happiness.

I would like to paint
The sea, the way it overlaps its last wave
And how it goes *shshsh* like a sleeping cat.

I would like to paint
The seagulls fighting over leftovers of food
How they acrobat in the air,
Up, down, left, right,
And how they squawk and squabble.

Marcus Jenkins (11)
Castlecroft Primary School, Castlecroft

On The Beach

I pick up the soft sand on my hand,
It tickles and runs through my fingers.
It glitters in the sun,
Looking up at everyone.
It feels gritty and rough when I rub it,
Then I let it go and it blows, blows, blows.

I pick up a cold rock in my hand,
It's all glittery from the sand,
It's rough and tough,
And lumpy and bumpy,
It's a multicoloured rock.

I pick up a cold shell in my hand,
Which has been lying there in the sand,
The outside ripples in waves,
Inside it is smooth, creamy white,
With an apricot tinge.

I pick up a starfish in my hand,
It's very delicate and amber-coloured,
Spotty and rough,
Underneath it is cream and peach,
I wonder where it has been
And what it has seen?

Emily Chappell (9)
Castlecroft Primary School, Castlecroft

Winter

Winter secretly crept by as the trees lay bare,
Winter quietly laid a white blanket over the skin of the rooftops,
Winter quickly laid ice over the bitterly cold puddles,
He breathed and turned the windows into frost.

Winter sprinkled silvery snowflakes about,
Winter decorated the sky with glistening snowballs,
Winter raced around under the transparent icicles,
He danced with the snowmen and laid a snow trail.

Naomi Saunders (11)
Castlecroft Primary School, Castlecroft

On The Beach

On the beach I pick up a shell,
It feels rough and jagged,
Some of them feel really tough,
Some have soft, silky insides.

On the beach I pick up some sand,
It feels very soft in my hand,
But if I rub it on my fingertips,
It feels crunchy and gritty.

On the beach I pick up a starfish,
It is very delicate, apricot-coloured,
Ivory and peach below,
Rough and bumpy to touch.

On the beach I pick up a pebble,
Some are rough and scratchy,
Some are smooth and silky,
Some are heavy and cold.

Chloe Hayes (9)
Castlecroft Primary School, Castlecroft

I Would Like To Paint . . .

I would like to paint the seagulls' hungriness
As they fight over dead crabs.

I would like to paint the rock pool's shimmer
And ripples in the sunlight.

I would like to paint the jellyfish bobbing up and down
And floating to the surface of the sea.

I would like to paint the sand's slurp when it is wet
And when it is dry, blow away.

I would like to paint the fish breathing bubbles
In the deep, blue, unknown sea.

I would like to paint the laughter and excitement
Of the children playing in the sand.

Katie Hemmings (11)
Castlecroft Primary School, Castlecroft

Winter

Winter charges past, eating the snow and spitting out the drops
he doesn't want,
Now he's running, splashing, splattering as he slows down,
spraying snow patterns,
Winter is walking, crushing everything, filling in the snow angel.

He breathes cold, frosty winter air, forcing people to shiver,
He gives the freezing crispy touch of snowflakes.
Winter is a wizard, he brews up a spell that tears leaves and
lets things freeze.

He tears, he falls, he freezes. He gets ready to kill,
One, two, three, four, five,
He lifts up his bony arm, gets ready to strike and . . .

He screams! He bellows! He shouts! He *dies,*
Yes! Winter's reign is over and spring is here,
The sun is out and daffodils grow,
And best of all children of all different ages
Come out and play.

Amy Burgwin (10)
Castlecroft Primary School, Castlecroft

Paintbox Colours

I will paint you a picture of the sea and the shore,
Of the greens and blues and yellows galore.

I will paint you a picture of the sand and the shore,
Of the golds and blues and more.

I will paint you a picture of the sun in the sky,
Of the reds and orange and yellow and blue.

I will paint you a picture of the shells.
The whites and reds and yellows and blue.

Ashley Abdislam (11)
Castlecroft Primary School, Castlecroft

I Would Like To Paint . . .

I would like to paint
The hugeness of the beach
As it stretches for miles and miles.

I would like to paint
The crabs toddling from side to side
As they snap their tiny claws.

I would like to paint
The boats sailing free
On the big, blue sea.

I would like to paint
The starfish stretching its arms
As if it is asleep - or is it awake?

I would like to paint the rocks
Sitting peacefully - doing nothing.

Laura Evans (11)
Castlecroft Primary School, Castlecroft

I Would Like To Paint . . .

Today I would like to paint the sea
Because it is so blue and calm.

Today I would like to paint the sun
Because it is so bright and yellow.

Today I would like to paint the sand
Because it feels so smooth and hard.

Today I would like to paint crabs
Because I can hear them moving in the shell.

Today I would like to paint the rocks
Because they look so simple
And feel so rough.

Devaraaj Nahar (11)
Castlecroft Primary School, Castlecroft

Drowning The World's Love

The wave came
Crashing, dashing.
Showing fury of Earth,
The water seeping on land,
Drowning the world's love.

The wave of darkness
Threatening the land,
Choking the golden sand,
Drowning the world's love.

Now they ask us why.
Why us Lord?
Your fury is seen.
Please show your forgiveness,
You drowned the world's love.

Jack Paskin (9)
Christ Church CE Primary School, Coseley

The Tsunami

It crashed.
It banged.
It took a chunk out of the world.
All I saw that day was terror growing in the waves.

It crashed.
It banged.
It took away part of this world.
What is to become of us in this world?

It crashed.
It banged.
Now I still ask the question 'Why us?' from this day on.

Katy Clifford-Sheldon (10)
Christ Church CE Primary School, Coseley

A Wave That Destroyed People's Lives!

It was a calm, peaceful morning and everyone was happy playing.

Then! It happened, something had brought a tsunami.

The immense wave roared like a tiger.
'It pulled me back.'
'I am badly hurt.'
The beautiful day became horrific.

Why, why, why!

My daughter and husband haven't been found.
I lost my home as it smashed right through.

The gargantuan wave took a huge bite from the world
And stretched families' lives.

Why us?

Katie Louise Nock (9)
Christ Church CE Primary School, Coseley

The Wave Of Death

The wave of death, the wave of death
Struck on the calm, peaceful land.
The silence turned to screams as buildings gradually plunged
to the ground.
The wave of death, the wave of death
Slaughtering innocent countries,
Gobbling them up in its perishing jaws.
People sleeping, people eating, all were washed away.
The wave of death, the wave of death
Taking out its anger on people who don't deserve it,
Leaving people questioning if their relatives and friends are still alive.
As they ask the question, 'Why?'

Shellie Noakes (10)
Christ Church CE Primary School, Coseley

The Tsunami Attack

Still, black, silent.
Then.
Crash!
Nothing else but the tsunami attack.
It was coming and we could see God
Face to face.
We wondered why the action-packed shock
Was here.
The waves were rushing across the villages not
Even pausing for a breath.

We saw God's fury face to face.
The blanket of waves was not soft
Or warming at all.
We saw God's fury face to face.
Trapped, trapped, stranded under sea.
Is this a dream?

No!
The question behind all this is,
Why?

Vinny Johnson (9)
Christ Church CE Primary School, Coseley

The Day Of Devastation

On that fateful day T remendous waves swallowed Asia.
The gigantic waves S mashed anything in its path.
The powerful beast is U nmatchable in any force.
The first clash only N ipped at the land.
The second slam tore A way the land at shocking speeds.
The third blow M ight be the last . . . for a few minutes!
All my family lost I n the flood, please help us.

Ross Timmins (11)
Christ Church CE Primary School, Coseley

Tsunami Verse

Calm,
Relaxed
Then *crash,* it hit
The sea took over
An earthquake spoke of its anger
A monstrous wave, clashing with buildings
Fighting with villages
Demolished, destroyed
Millions homeless, millions lost,
What?
What will they do?

Dread,
Upset
An immense wave loomed above
Then plunged down on us,
Leaving us with nothing
Our pain
Our fear
What?
What will we do?

Hope,
Pray
Things will be OK
This fatal moment
I await my saviour,
My fortune,
I need it
But what,
What will I do?

Jessica Nightingale (11)
Christ Church CE Primary School, Coseley

Lila

'Lila! Lila!'
Is that my family
Calling, calling for me,
Trying to find me?
But I am trapped,
Caught up in a web of horror and torment.
It's all the sea's fault.
'Why?
Why?
Why?' is all I ask.

'Lila! Lila!'
Don't give up.
Please don't give up.
That's all my heart is screaming for.
Yet in my mind, all that is there is a scar.
A picture engraved,
Etched into my memory.
It stays there, unable to move.
The scar of a magnificent sapphire-blue wave.

'Lila! Lila!'
Keep searching.
Keep scouring the land for me.
Just please, please save me.
For years and years to come
A nightmare of this terrible event will flash across my life,
Flooding my heart with pain.
The smell of death will keep wafting up my nostrils,
Torturing me.
Teasing me.
I want all this to be a dream.
But it is real,
As real as this hell engulfing the land.

'Lila! Lila!'
Please God, please save me.
I will do anything.
I'll be as good as an angel sent from Heaven.
I'll be a blessing upon all people.
I'll be a prayer worth a thousand words.
Just please, please keep holding onto my life.

'Lila! Lila!'
The voice of a searching soul is crying out my name,
I fight to hear the voice of my saviour,
But the raging noise of the tsunami is all I hear,
Echoing through my mind
As I lie trapped in my inky black prison.
Please, please find me
Before all hope washes away.
And please answer my forever-unanswered question,
Why?

'Lila! Lila!'
My soul is drifting, drifting away,
As my strength fades I struggle to sustain my life.
I want to escape.
I want to live.
I don't want to die.
So please, please find me.
Save me from this watery tomb.

Let me live to ask my forever-unanswered question,
Why?

Chelsea Davies (10)
Christ Church CE Primary School, Coseley

Tsunami

A huge wave wall approaching,
Coming closer, closer, closer,
Eventually the sea gnawed at the helpless villagers,
Ripping buildings down to shreds,
Smashing, gnawing, tearing,
An unwelcome guest swaying in and out of houses
through windows and doors,
Sweeping people in its wake
Floating bodies everywhere,
Homes wrecked,
People dead,
Survivors with nowhere to go.

What are we going to do?
Where are we going to go?
Why us?

Ben Rubery (10)
Christ Church CE Primary School, Coseley

Tsunami Poem

Children playing with little
notice of the gigantic wave,
about to hit.
All calm on the beach.
With little notice of the
gigantic wave.

Crash! The sea came blasting in
without any warning.
The sea split up in
different directions.
Bodies, trees, houses, cars
passing through.
No warning,
no care,
all I ask is, 'Why, why us?'

Ryan Hughes (10)
Christ Church CE Primary School, Coseley

Why?

Nature's time bomb stealing lives
Children screaming with pain,
Why them?
Gargantuan waves always coming
Sea moving back, waiting to pounce
Why them?

Waves grasping sleeping buildings
People sinking in mud,
Why them?
Crushing waves tearing down houses
People facing death
Why them?

Waves swamping homes
Some survived.
Why so many dead?
All this happened in Asia
While we ask the question, 'Why?'

William Swansborough-Aston (9)
Christ Church CE Primary School, Coseley

The Tsunami

It crashed over the sleeping land, stealing people's lives,
It chomped at the land leaving crumbs behind.

All of a sudden our land was swept away,
Into the arms of this humungous wave.

Our country was wiped off the map,
A chunk out of the world.

This would take some time to forget about,
But we still ask, 'Why us? Why us?

Where is our Saviour?'

Jordan Parkes (10)
Christ Church CE Primary School, Coseley

But Why?

It was the 26th December 2004, the disaster struck
the people of Sri Lanka
were waking up to a disaster
the sea was slipping on and off the shore.
Then in a moment it was silent to a baby's cry.
But still we ask, 'Why us?'

It kept on going, people were shouting and screaming,
'It's coming again!'
Why did it hurt us? What did we do wrong?
So many questions - but only silence,
cries of pain, 'We need help,'
the only thing that is left is bodyboards with dead, missing, or
found alive,
But we still ask, 'Why us?'

I pray for hope, life and care,
I pray I'll find my friends and family,
I pray that the terrible wave will not kill anymore.

But why?

Sophie Bolton (9)
Christ Church CE Primary School, Coseley

Tsunami

T he prodigious wave swallowed us all.
S ome survived the colossal wall of water,
It's U nimaginable that some of us are okay,
N eedy families are in need of food and water,
A gargantuan wave smashed down the walls
M any people ran and screamed as an earthquake rocked Asia.
I asked, 'Why us?'

Tom Nicklin & Sam Pitt (10)
Christ Church CE Primary School, Coseley

The Biggest Disaster

On December 26th 2004 there was a calm sea in the Indian Ocean
until *Crash!* The tsunami had struck.
As the goliath wave pounced onto Sri Lanka, people were screaming
and shouting for help.
The monstrous wave was a time bomb waiting to explode
screaming, shouting.
'It's coming again,' people shouted as the wave pushed
buildings to the ground.
The tsunami - the biggest disaster to strike the Earth.
Thousands of people died that day, still dying.
Thousands of people missing.
Tsunami, the biggest disaster to strike the Earth.

But we still ask,
'Why?'

Laura Hickman (10)
Christ Church CE Primary School, Coseley

The Tsunami

The tsunami bombed down upon the land as thousands
ran for their lives.
Little babies sleeping swept out as the wave crashed
down on the beach.
People relaxing lost their lives.
No one knew but it was too late.
Leaving destruction behind, nothing left, completely
wiped off the map.

But there's still one question

Why?

Thomas Barratt (9)
Christ Church CE Primary School, Coseley

Tsunami (Set In India)

There was a calm sea on December 26th 2004,
It was as if nothing was happening,
Until suddenly the plates of the Earth started playing in the
Indian Ocean.
One shot up, and one shot down encouraging an amazing force out of
Which rose a gargantuan wave.
It was the start of the tsunami.
The wave of death had risen.

I was lying on a beach minding my own business when I saw a
Monstrous wave, it was enormous.
I started running as fast as I could.
I felt as if it was extraordinary because it was.
I thought, *what is happening?*
Do you know?
There was my best friend in his house when the tsunami struck,
He said it didn't knock, it just came storming in.
The colossal wave devoured the house.
He was picked up by the wave.
The wave of death had struck.

The king-sized bed of water was a nightmare on the Earth,
And I'm telling you it must have been an unpleasant one.
Millions of people had died, not just in this country but in others.
We all ask, 'God, why us, why does Your fury have to strike us?'
All we ask is the question, 'Why?'
The wave of death has struck us.
Why oh why us?

Bradley Norton (9)
Christ Church CE Primary School, Coseley

When The Tsunami Struck

When the tsunami struck
Underneath the sea
It took away people's lives, their children
And made their friends and family hurt.

Children crying
Reaching out for love
Love that has been lost
Lost in what are now remains.

Two clashes underneath the sea
Caused the goliath wave
To chew up, spit out and even swallow
Many people's lives, home and children.

When the tsunami struck
Underneath the perfect seabed,
It destroyed people's hopes and dreams.

When the tsunami struck,
It did not tell me it was coming,
It just came
With a roar, a rush and a pounce,
It now rests
On its destroyed seabed.

And all it leaves behind
Is a broken world of emptiness.

Now the people
Who have lost loved ones
Cry out for love
And love is all they ask for.

Charlie-Ann Hollington (10)
Christ Church CE Primary School, Coseley

The Wave, The Wave!

People lying on a beach,
Turned to death at others' feet.
At first people thought it was no threat.
But the wave,
The wave,
The wave had come
Splishing, splashing in a pool
It was in the morning.
Now the immense waves hit,
Lots were missing, under bricks.
But the wave,
The wave,
The wave has panicked people
Now loved ones are lost and gone
Forever
The wave,
The wave.

Connor Schofield (11)
Christ Church CE Primary School, Coseley

The Deadly Nightmare

It was peaceful, quiet and then it came,
This gigantic, mighty, deadly wave.
The sea swallowed up thousands of homes and lives,
Then it threatened people to run, run for their lives,
And if they didn't, to say their goodbyes.

The waves coming up, up and up
Leaving us abandoned, nothing to hold,
Not even a shoulder to cry on.
Begging for help, begging for this nightmare to end.
But this was not a dream, this was reality
That leaves a big, gaping scar!

Bethany Davies (10)
Christ Church CE Primary School, Coseley

We Will Remember

It was morning all quiet and still,
Until the Earth began to shake
And then they knew the king cobra had awakened from its bed,
No one was expecting it,
They all started to shout.

It stood up looking over the people,
And then it decided what to do.
It struck up the beach,
Pulling everything back, not letting anything go
Drifting away, drifting away until it had gone.

All that's left now is dirt and bricks from fields and buildings,
And all they ask is, 'Why us?'
Does anyone know the answer?

April Dale (10)
Christ Church CE Primary School, Coseley

End Of A Year

A normal day in Indonesia,
Survival had just got a little bit easier,
But all that was happening today was running and screaming,
Everyone was either being hurt or running and wheezing,
It took down buildings, swept people off their feet,
Amazing things were flying across the sky,
A window, a table, maybe a seat,
Running and screaming, hurting and wheezing,
It was like a giant too big to stop it,
It wasn't taking it bit by bit,
But chunk by chunk,
What have they done to receive this pain, fury and strife?
Many people have lost all and many their life,
Why did the tsunami pick that day?
Many died on Boxing Day.

Elliot Rollason (10)
Christ Church CE Primary School, Coseley

It

First of all the sea rolled back, back to where it came from,
But then,
Back it came as a huge tidal wave,
Smack! The thing hit the innocent land,
Bang! The impact was too much to bear.

Then I saw it,
A body just floating by,
Then I saw more,
More and more and more,
Smack! the thing hit the innocent land,
Bang! The impact was too much to bear.

Grabbing onto a pole, I watched life pass me by,
But the question we all must ask,
Is the question,
Why?

Grace Swansborough-Aston (11)
Christ Church CE Primary School, Coseley

The Horror

This is a poem about a broken land,
An almighty surge destroying
Everything, like a bomb hitting land.

Waves rolled lives upside down
As everything whirled round and round.
Water rose like a hot air balloon
As the wind howled like a feisty baboon.

Our emotions are speechless, we cannot
Speak a word, for the silence is never-ending
But my life is heard.

But behind this thought there is a question,
The question is, why us?

Elise Roberts (9)
Christ Church CE Primary School, Coseley

The Disaster

Once upon a time
Children were playing,
Adults were sunbathing,
People were sleeping
And eating and waking,
And all was calm
And *then* out of the blue,
The disaster struck like a king cobra,
Like a giant drawing breath,
Taking a chunk out of the world,
The waves swallowing people's homes and lives forever,
A great wall of water destroying the beautiful area,
We had no warning
This is not a dream, we have paid the price.
Once upon a time
Children were playing,
Adults were sunbathing,
And all was calm.

Megan Lane (10)
Christ Church CE Primary School, Coseley

The Tsunami

People lying on the beach not aware the wave would come,
They saw the magnificent waves and thought, *not a threat.*
The people ran but they had nowhere to go from the huge wave.
The people saw it, the huge wave.
Astonished at what they saw, the people, terrified, shivered with fear.
After the wave, people penniless, the wave had gobbled the villages.

Ashley Mattey (9)
Christ Church CE Primary School, Coseley

The Destroyed Little Villages

It was morning,
The morning that would be remembered forever.
The people of the quiet little villages,
Slept, ate breakfast and were sunbathing.

The quiet little villages.

While underneath the world below the plates moved
They dashed together and, *boom,* it happened.
The wave opened its jaws and sucked up all the villages.
In one second the millions of people were dead.

The destroyed little villages.

People were screaming for help,
Trying to hold onto buildings,
Trying to hold onto their children,
Trying to hold onto their belongings,
But it didn't work, it all went.

The destroyed little villages.

Their lives had gone, destroyed.
'How could it happen?' people asked.
From this day, my town, my village won't be on the map anymore.

The destroyed little villages.

Many people are crying out loud,
'Why was it us, what did we do?
Help, please help!' they say out loud.
They cry and cry.

The poor destroyed little villages.

Elle Fletcher (9)
Christ Church CE Primary School, Coseley

Tsunami Disaster

It was a normal day,
I was at the beach
When suddenly it struck,
Killing innocent people,
'Why?' I ask.

Towns, villages, all badly destroyed,
People's lives shattered.
This huge wave had swallowed
People and their homes.
'Why us?' I ask.

I am concerned how two plates
Can create such hurt and disaster,
People's sons, daughters and relatives
All dead, the question is,
'Why us?' we ask.

Abigail Devison (11)
Christ Church CE Primary School, Coseley

Tsunami

T ransgressor taking an extensive chunk out of the world,
S tealing lives from the coast,
U seless people run for their lives as the rapid wave haunts them.
N o one could stop the monstrous waves
A bhorrent innocent people.
M aintaining its dreadful horror.
I t is like a nuclear bomb waiting to go off.

Christopher Harris (11)
Christ Church CE Primary School, Coseley

The Tsunami Terror Came

The tsunami terror came
and stole the lives of many.
The enormous wave swallowed up the land.
The cry of death echoes all around.
The tsunami terror came.

The tsunami terror came
and stole the lives of many.
Why?
Why the tragic wave?
Why?
Families lost,
lost to the sea.
The tsunami terror came
and stole the lives of many.

The tsunami terror came
and stole the lives of many.
The enormous wave swallowed up the land.
The cry of death echoes all around.
The tsunami terror came.

Natalie Rowley (11)
Christ Church CE Primary School, Coseley

The Tsunami

The gigantic wall of water ran through villages,
Not letting anything survive in its way.

We saw the fury of God,
We saw it face to face.

We couldn't help, it was so quick.

We saw the fury of God,
We saw it face to face.

People clung to each other not wanting to let go.

We saw the fury of God,
We saw it face to face.

'Why us?' people cried while clinging to their children.

We saw the fury of God,
We saw it face to face.

Heartbroken families full with tears.

They saw the fury of God,
They saw it face to face.

Taylor Bagley (9)
Christ Church CE Primary School, Coseley

The Tsunami Disaster

It was a calm sunny day, the sea was as calm as always,
It was early in the morning and many people were sunbathing,
Or swimming or some still asleep.
The sea pulled away showing the whole beach
Making a great titanic-sized wave form.

Death, death, death.

As the wave rose, people ran and screamed.
It was like it was following them crashing, ripping and
Obliterating buildings.
It was killing, drowning innocent people and tourists.
They had no warning, no equipment.

Death, death, death.

It struck like lightning on a fork except it was on land with water,
Oh death, death, death.
Why did it hit them? Why? Why? Why?

Ryan Beasley (10)
Christ Church CE Primary School, Coseley

Tsunami

The calm, peaceful sea swaying here and there,
Lovely trees softly blow in the breeze.
Kind people celebrate Christmas as joy runs around the village,
For all they have will soon be gone.

For in the sea a small disaster,
The earthquake was now the master.
A devilish wave heads their way,
It sprints, it runs like a bullet from a gun.
As it draws closer, the people run from the evil wave.

A lady screams, her forgotten dreams,
As a car flees like you and me.
The waves jump, kick and punch, dragging the people away,
For all the people ran away because Mother Nature had betrayed.

This all started Boxing Day when the hellish wave took them away,
So bow your heads and pray for the people who died that day,
Just hope one day there is a way to pay back the people on that day.

Ian Baugh (11)
Christ Church CE Primary School, Coseley

The Day The Tsunami Struck

The grey, murky sea bullied people who cried for help.
The water went berserk and flattened their city.
Water overtook and barged its way beyond the palm trees.
It killed loved ones who didn't deserve to die.
The wave jumped on the city like a tiger leaping out.
It struck like lightning in horror.

Their homes were ripped apart like a piece of paper.
The sand got carried in by the killer wave.
The beach was chewed away by the terrifying sea.
The cars were floating away like boats down a stream.
There were clothes riddling down the great monstrous sea.
There were people's possessions running away from them.

There is nothing left of the city, only floods.
They are trying to find loved ones from under the twigs and fences that have been washed away.
What has happened to the beloved city?
It has swiped people's lives away forever.
Why should families suffer in this way?
No one knows, only God.

Laura Meredith (11)
Christ Church CE Primary School, Coseley

Tsunami

The water struck dragging us by our hand
And knee out to the roaring sea.
Smashing, crashing, punching through the buildings,
Water thrusting forwards and forwards,
Waves getting higher and higher,
People never knew what was going to happen.

Water ramming, crashing,
Water whaling, shoving, attacking,
Clapping, squeezing, jamming.
People screaming, crying, drowning,
People murdered lying around,
Children wondering looking around,
People shouting for help.

People cramming up,
People washed away,
Running for their lives, but they're too late.
The wave has got those people,
Trying to get to their families,
But they can't find them,
No one for them.

Angry, innocent people that have done no harm
Are gone for no reason, no reason at all.
Now they are alone, heartbroken people.

Serena Sheamar (11)
Christ Church CE Primary School, Coseley

Why

The two rock plates had rubbed each other,
Like two pieces of sandpaper.
It caused a tsunami,
The wave gradually ripped up the ocean.

It had reached its speed up to 500 miles per hour,
The bloodthirsty wave was heading at everything in its path,
Nothing could have stopped this great disaster,
Not even Mother Nature,
Nothing.

The people they all live in fear now,
Most of them have lost everything, including their families.
Now it's a struggle to put their lives back together,
Still asking themselves why? Why?

That day well over 150,000 people died,
Most still had a whole life ahead of them.
I was speechless that day,
That day was a disaster.

The world should never forget the day nature showed us
What she could do, and the respect she demands.
By showing us that no building, or person can be stronger than her,
Than the power she possesses
That day Mother Nature ripped out a piece of everybody's heart,
Including mine.

Chad Riley (10)
Christ Church CE Primary School, Coseley

When The Tsunami Struck

All of a sudden the musky, angry sea
Was taking over the panicking town,
Forcing through the homes,
Drowning people.

Whooshing at them, destroying them,
Tearing families apart,
The tsunami raided
The cities and lands.

The buildings and homes were screeching
For help from their owners,
The wave went berserk at their crying buildings
And smashed them more.

The petrifying wave was bullying the terrified people.
It carried them out to the empty world,
Taking them out the destroying sea.

The wave roared like an angry tiger,
The wave clawed the city
Into tiny pieces.

Stephanie Anslow (11)
Christ Church CE Primary School, Coseley

The Fire Poem

Crackle, pop goes the little fire
Whoosh, goes the massive flame
Then it burns up all the little trees
Sizzle, fizzle, bang and *whistle.*

Fire turns the trees to ashes
Hear it crunch and click
Sparks fly everywhere
When the fire goes out it turns into a clump of powder
Shhh.

Adam Pipes (10)
Edge Hill Junior School, Stapenhill

Spring

Spring is a great time for children
Because there's so much to see
Like buds and flowers and also animals
Boys and girls, boys and girls chase a bumblebee.

Spring is a great time for animals
Lambs bounce around the field
Pets lap up all of their food
And cows have calves to shield.

Spring is a fantastic time for flowers
Daffodils, tulips and roses
Children play in the garden all day
And wet each other with hoses.

Spring is a great time for children
Because there's so much to see
Spring is a great time for everyone
Spring is a great time for me.

Hannah Timson (7)
Edge Hill Junior School, Stapenhill

The Seasons

Flowers blossom in the spring
And all the birds will talk and sing.

In the summer we all like to play
And have an ice cream on a sunny day.

In the autumn leaves turn yellow
And blow off the trees in the autumn below.

A white frosty morning in the sky
Tells us that winter is nigh.

All these seasons we can see
How beautiful the world can be.

Annie Stonehouse-Burt (9)
Edge Hill Junior School, Stapenhill

The Race

Shuffle, shuffle as he goes to the start line,
The gun goes bang and off we go,
As we go the gravel goes crunch, scrunch,
We jump the first hurdle,
As we hit the ground there's a boom,
We start running again,
Whoosh goes the wind speeding past me,
It starts to rain,
Splash as we go through a puddle,
The finish line is in front,
The crowd rattles and cheers,
And horns are squealing.

Oliver Hill (9)
Edge Hill Junior School, Stapenhill

My Cat

My cat is furry and cute,
It likes to sniff at my boot.
My cat likes to know where I've been,
(Just in case I've seen the Queen.)

My cat likes to play tinkle ball,
He flicks it fast down the hall.
When it's lost under the chair,
He likes to sit and just stare.

I love my cat and he loves me,
He has a cuddle on my knee.
When it's time to go to bed,
He sits on my pillow next to my head.

Dominique Kniveton (8)
Edge Hill Junior School, Stapenhill

Onomatopoeia

Slip, slop raindrop
Drizzling onto the windowpane
Pitter-patter, splatter, cracker
Here comes raindrops again.

Tick-tock of the clock
Swinging side to side
Splitter, splatter, splitter, splatter
It's coming down your drive.

Shannon Davis (9)
Edge Hill Junior School, Stapenhill

Home And Away

Buzz, buzz went the bee as he flew around the room,
Miaow, miaow went the cat as she sat by the broom.
Swish, swish went the curtains as the wind blew,
'Wow!' said the prince looking at the view.

Tick-tock went the clock on the bare wall,
Clip-clop went the shoes at the palace ball.
Pop! went the balloon when the people were having fun,
Tinkle, tinkle went the bell as they began to run.

Amy Lewis (9)
Edge Hill Junior School, Stapenhill

Natural Sounds

Listen to the clock going tick-tock, tick-tock,
Listen to the pots and pans, clitter, clatter,
The leaves outside rustle on the floor,
The bee on the table goes buzz, buzz,
But among the leaves of the trees outside,
In the silence of the wind an eagle flies by.

Terri-Ann Butcher (10)
Edge Hill Junior School, Stapenhill

The Wind

The wind roars like a lion at everyone
It will only stop when its job is done
Howling, blowing, roaring, it's devastating
The screaming noise is manipulating.

Sometimes the wind blows without a care
The bellowing lion causes nightmares
Or sometimes the beast is gentle
And could not blow away a lentil.

The wind can conjure up tornados or even hurricanes
It causes problems for aeroplanes
The lion stalks its prey
Day after day.

It could blow away a house for miles
Or knock down a wood stockpile
But on a sunny warm day it's great to feel a breeze
And relax as everything is at ease.

Ashley Cockrill (11)
Highfields Primary School, Burntwood

World War II Poem

Bombs are dropping all around, flying from each direction,
Soldiers choosing guns from all selection.

Lots of planes shooting like guns
With terrified mums.

With dads leaving precious mums and children
Going to war to win the battle for England.

Some come back, some don't
Leaving their precious wives and children.

Hayley Caudren (10)
Highfields Primary School, Burntwood

The Day The Tsunami Came

An earthquake came from faraway seas,
Destroying all the plants and trees.
All that was left were panic and fear,
Screaming and shouting were all you could hear.

People were buried in great big graves,
About a dozen in each because of the wave,
Down on their knees the survivors prayed
For the thousands of people that died that day.

Food and aid supplies were running short,
While other countries gave support.
Three minutes' silence was given for the day
When the waves came in further than the bay.

We remember these people,
We shout it from the highest steeple,
People out there want a clean drink
When we can get one from the sink.

Fern Simkins (10)
Highfields Primary School, Burntwood

Colour Poem

When I think of the colour green,
I think of the big things that I've seen.

When I think of very bright red,
All I want to do is lie there in bed.

When I see the colour yellow,
I act like a jolly good fellow.

When I think of the colour blue,
I want an arty afternoon with very sticky glue.

When I think of the colour brown,
I think of the people that have let me down.

When I think of the colour white,
I want to fly a very big kite.

Sam Farmer (10)
Highfields Primary School, Burntwood

Rumble And Tumble In The Jungle

All so quiet you can't hear a sound,
No vibrations on the ground.
But then suddenly a snake comes out of the trees,
And the cheeky monkeys copy the chimpanzees

Elephants feed themselves with their trunks,
Guess who's on their backs?
A group of monkeys.
All so quiet you cannot hear a sound,
But them on the ground . . .

A tribe of monkeys swinging through the trees,
Followed by the chimpanzees.
The snakes get funky and do a whirl,
Let's do the same and a twirl.

They swing into their homes,
And are as silent as garden gnomes.
They have gone to their beds
To rest their sleepy heads.
Night, night in the rumbly, tumbly jungle.
Rumble and tumble in the jungle.

Heather Evans (10)
Highfields Primary School, Burntwood

The Asian Disaster

People celebrating, Boxing Day had nearly passed,
The angry wave ravaged,
Making this a day to last,
Crying with fear because of the hungry wave,
Hoping to themselves that they would be saved.

More than 100,000 lives were taken that day,
Because the tidal wave crashed on the bay,
People left with hunger and starvation,
While other people are suffering with dehydration.
We are so lucky can't you see?
So lucky that it wasn't our sea.

Morgan Nash (10)
Highfields Primary School, Burntwood

A Day Walking On The Beach

The tide is out, I'm feeling relaxed,
It's so hot here you could burn candle wax,
The sky is a wonderful sapphire-blue,
The sea is turquoise, the sand looks brand new.

The sun is hot, the air is clear,
I put on your postcard, 'Wish you were here.'
Children making sandcastles all over the place,
Having lots of fun, a smile on their face.

There're shells in the sand, I put one close to my ear,
I listen very carefully, the sea is what I hear.
Licking an ice cream is cool on my tongue.
Hold on till I'm back, it won't be long.

The day is near its end, the sun is going down,
After such a great day, no need for a frown.
My footprints leave indents all over the sand,
I have a present here for you in my hand.

The tide is out, I'm feeling relaxed,
It's so hot here, you could burn candle wax,
The sky is wonderful with a ruby-red hue,
The sea looks on fire, the sand looks brand new.

The beach has become deserted,
The ruby-red sky has set,
The fiery sea is sleeping,
A view you can't forget.

Joanne Howell (10)
Highfields Primary School, Burntwood

The Boxing Day Tsunami

The day of celebration had just passed,
When under the sea, the rocks just clashed
And the waves they caused were
Moving so fast they seemed to blur.
Tourists scrambled to their feet,
As the waves covered their seats.

Livestock running from their cage,
Hitting people of a young age.
Buildings crumbled like a sandcastle,
Causing a lot of hassle.

Corpses lay row by row,
Each body lay toe to toe,
Blankets covered dead individuals,
The air was echoing with lots of calls.

Aid planes flying through the air,
People running stopped and stared.
Aren't we lucky we weren't harmed?
Luckily the waves were calmed.

Money landing in a box,
At least enough for a pair of socks.
None of the words in the thesaurus
Can describe what we saw before us.

Ashley Austin (11)
Highfields Primary School, Burntwood

The Boxing Day Disaster

The Earth cracked like a glass,
A massive wave that people couldn't pass,
Leaving hardly any survivors,
Not even deep sea divers.

Homes were lost, crumbled and washed away,
Nobody could have predicted this fateful day,
The awful end to a prosperous year,
The only emotions are sadness and fear.

The survivors pray down on their knees
In the hope that someone will hear their pleas,
The wave was massive,
It most definitely was not passive.

The wave gave people a nasty fright,
Whilst we were sleeping all through the night.

Nikki Mawson (11)
Highfields Primary School, Burntwood

Happiness Is All Around

Happiness is as yellow as the sun sparkling
in the sky as if saying hello.
Happiness sounds like little birds chirping
in the early morning on a spring day.
Happiness tastes like sweet strawberries
covered in sugar and cream.
Happiness smells like candyfloss and toffee apples
at a funfair on a summer's day.
Happiness looks like a sunny day on a picnic
with children laughing and having fun.
Happiness makes you feel joyful and bouncy inside
and wanting to help everyone.
Happiness reminds me of being snuggled up in my bed
with my dog, watching television.

Abigail Moorhouse (9)
Highfields Primary School, Burntwood

The War

The bombs are dropping through the air,
People running here and there,
People getting hit by bullets,
Falling into big, big turrets.

All you can see is the gleaming orange fire,
Using all their power that the public desire,
Pouncing from battlefield to battlefield,
As the blows are dealed

Bombs and gunfire heard in the distance,
Soldiers fighting for their resistance,
Aircraft carriers on their way,
With Harrier jump jets here to stay.

As the war is coming to an end,
Civilians are left with nothing,
Soldiers fought for our freedom,
And this is how we remember them.

Tom Ryder (11)
Highfields Primary School, Burntwood

Happiness Poem

Happiness is yellow like a beautiful spring day
with the sun shining and the flowers blooming.
Happiness sounds like birds chirping and bees buzzing
on a sunny day.
Happiness tastes like juicy strawberries and raspberries.
Happiness smells like sweet candyfloss and toffee apples
bought on a summer's day.
Happiness looks like beautiful waterfalls
and pretty coloured butterflies.
Happiness feels all warm and snug when it's cold outside
and warm inside.
Happiness reminds me of holidays with my family.

Sofie Osman (10)
Highfields Primary School, Burntwood

A Blizzard Is An Eagle

A blizzard is a descending eagle,
Diving at its prey,
The snow is like an eagle's wing,
Covering a trembling mouse.
Sparkling snow covers everything,
Every tree and every house.

The cold is sharp like an eagle's beak,
Pecking its prey, making it weak,
Icicles hanging like sharp claws,
Making us want to stay indoors.
Frost and ice are cold and biting,
So are the eagle's claws scratching and fighting.

The whipping wind howls and spins,
Like a giant eagle flapping its wings,
The trees bend as fences fall,
As the giant bird comes to call.
Everything's quiet and we are at rest,
The blizzard eagle's flown back to its nest.

Eleanor Taylor (9)
Highfields Primary School, Burntwood

A Poem On War

People worried, what a scare,
When their families died they couldn't bear,
No more money, not even sweets,
No more proper dinners, no more treats.

Bombs dropping here and there,
Some people thought war wasn't fair.
Curfews were given,
While the battle was raging the tanks were driven.

The air raid siren rang out loud,
While German bombers bombed our ground,
As people ran to their homes,
There was no contact because there were no phones.

Ashleigh McLeod (10)
Highfields Primary School, Burntwood

The Eagle

The lava gusting out of a volcano,
Just like flinging open a door,
Soon their will be lava sliding around,
Just like a snake slipping under each floorboard.

Now the lava is furious,
Just like a vicious eagle,
Spurting up in the sky,
Glistening and gleaming way up high.

Suddenly, the lava is quietly slithering under each floorboard,
People are pushing and screaming everywhere
Flames are flickering with a nasty glare,
There's nothing left, not even an ant.

Lava is fuming with fire,
Killing anything, anywhere in the eagle's sight,
Just like the eagle catching its prey,
All you can do is run, run, run, run.
Now the eagle's gone back to its nest,
Everybody will remember this dread.

Ashley Bird (10)
Highfields Primary School, Burntwood

Happiness Poem

Happiness is like love in the sky,
It never breaks if people die.
Happiness makes people as happy as sunshine.
Happiness is people's power of divine,
As it is the colour green as the nice, lovely grass.
It sounds like someone holding a lovely brass.
Happiness tastes like a nice, juicy apple,
It smells like lovely perfume, as pretty as a rose.
Happiness looks like a big smiley face.
Happiness feels like a soft dog's fur.
Happiness makes me think of a dove flying in the air.

Emma Fielding (9)
Highfields Primary School, Burntwood

The Four Seasons

Spring is a month of happiness,
But sadly the leaves make a mess,
Spring is like a sweet bunny
With the buzzing bees making honey.

The birds sing so softly and so sweetly,
As the children of the nursery start to meet,
It's like a warm and sunny beach.

Whereas winter is like a squelchy leech,
Sucking and squeezing at your blood
As the soft soil turns to mud.

The snow is as heavy as a 100 ton block,
As the ships sail out from the dock.
And summer is a hot and joyful time
When people have barbecues and drink wine.

Sophie Dowson (11)
Highfields Primary School, Burntwood

Love Is Pink

Love is pink like a red rose
Blooming in the sunlight.
Love sounds like a bird high in the trees
Singing day and night.

Love tastes like a delicious sweet
Melting slowly in your mouth.
Love smells like a box of chocolates
Just been opened.

Love looks like the sun on a sunny day
Beaming through the clouds.

Love feels like a cocktail being slowly stirred
On a cruise.
Love reminds me of a heart
Flying high in the sky.

Beverley-Jane Cole (11)
Highfields Primary School, Burntwood

Rain Of Tears

I think the rain is just God's tears,
It consumes you with your greatest fears,
The tears make everything sulky and wet,
It will take a long time for these tears to set.

The plants are growing thanks to the rain,
The animals are drowning, going through pain,
What did we do to make God this sad?
It must have been unpleasant, for rain this bad.

From the drip on your nose to the patter on your feet,
It stomps like a dinosaur and makes you jump out of your seat,
God is spreading pain and fear,
For the patter of death is drawing near.

God is crying mayhem and that's all I can say,
Now God is the predator and we're the prey,
For this is the way the world goes round,
It is so loud you are deafened by the sound.

Now the rain has come to a stop,
There was no rain, not even a drop,
Now the season of summer is drawing near,
The animals come out, not consumed by fear.

Daniel Newbury (11)
Highfields Primary School, Burntwood

The Scorpion King

The scorpion king lying around as quiet as a cloud,
A scorpion is a deadly creature waiting for its prey at any moment,
And a scorpion can stay where it is all day if it catches its prey,
And it doesn't matter it can stay there all day,
Only if it catches its prey
And it doesn't need water for thousands of days.

Jonathon Hancox (10)
Highfields Primary School, Burntwood

The Futility Of War

Bombs start to drop from planes above,
Symbolic of so much hate, not love.
Dropped to cause mass devastation,
So much havoc caused through the nation.

Now as those missiles meet with the ground,
All that is chaos starts to resound.
People screaming here and there,
They have no time to waste . . . to spare.

Running, trying to hide, to find a shelter,
They attack this time, everyone felt her
The mood below turns from happy to sad,
The reason for war is they all seem mad.

One after the other the explosions boom,
Explosive enough to demolish the room,
They all seem to go on for hours without care,
Then a sudden deathly silence fills the air.

Filled with fear, people start to reappear,
Witness the wreckage, stop, look and listen,
But what people feel more and more,
The great sense of futility of war.

The men go without a trace,
They quickly pick up their pace,
The bombs are dropped without a care,
The children have no clothes, they are stripped bare.

Bethany Ford (10)
Highfields Primary School, Burntwood

The End Of The World

Everything is burning,
The apocalypse has begun,
Everything is burning,
Under the blazing hot sun.

People fleeing for their lives,
Sprinting through the land,
Looking for a place of safety,
Falling into the sand.

The apocalypse is a thundering dragon,
Crushing things in its way,
Killing people whatever age,
It's not like that today.

People trying to save their lives,
From Satan's vicious knives,
What did we do to make him this mad,
Because now he has made us miserable and sad?

Fireballs tearing through the skies,
Like two of Satan's flaming eyes,
Destroying the Earth bit by bit,
It's not the time to loaf about and sit.

The apocalypse is finally over,
But nothing is left, not even a three-leaved clover,
The disaster it has made,
Will never ever be dismayed.

Oliver Jones (10)
Highfields Primary School, Burntwood

School Teachers

The kids think teachers are slimy,
At St Peter's Primary,
But the register is unpleasant,
As it is taken by Mrs Pheasant,
She is a tall, sharp-tongued woman,
When you see her your belly starts to numb,
She sits down with the register in her hand,
'Duncan Brown,' she shouts with demand,
But then there is Mr Drover,
With his face looking like it had been turned over.
He is hesitant and faint-hearted,
And his nostrils are barely parted.
He is the one with the disgrace
Of indoctrinating science and space.
But then there's the teacher of English and maths,
And sometimes he has to cover crafts.
He snorts when he speaks,
And his stretched nose looks like an eagle's beak.
But then there's the teacher of RE,
But he would much rather be in charge of PE,
Because religion is his weakness,
And so is his neatness,
His clothes are as bedraggled as an old rag,
He misses half of his lessons outside having a fag.
But the head teacher is the most evil,
He is as mad as Evil Knevil,
He's got vampire teeth and a scouring grin,
And he smells like I don't know where he's been,
The kids think the teachers are slimy,
At St Peter's Primary.

Joe Henson (10)
Highfields Primary School, Burntwood

The Atmosphere Of World War II

The bombs are dropping,
As fast as a car.
Families are scared,
And trying to get far.

Soldiers getting hurt,
Fighting for us.
Families and wives have had,
Their close ones lost.

11th of 11th is when it all took place,
Germans killing English soldiers without any grace.
Buildings burning,
Stomachs churning,
The smell of smoke,
People's hearts broke.

Air raid sirens going off,
People running to the nearest stop.
We wear poppies to remember,
The war that ended on the 11th November.

People queuing for their rations,
This is the World War fashion.
Happiness turned all around,
And people's faces turned to frowns.

They did not know if they would survive,
They just kept fighting and risked their lives.

Victoria Penlington (10)
Highfields Primary School, Burntwood

Night-Time

It's the time of day where everything goes dark,
The creaking of the stairs, like the swings in the park,
The howling of the wind like a dog's rough bark,
And the screeches of the teenagers that lark.

Why is it that when you're awake,
You're scared of the sounds that you make?
The quacking of the ducks in the nearby lake,
I'm waiting for the light, how long does it take?

It's as dark as a black volcano rock,
Peeping around, everywhere you look,
Your jumper is a monster,
Don't take a second look.

Everything is chilly, like an ice cube straight from the freezer,
This is scary, let's pause for a breather,
The sun now rises like a pie out of the oven,
The house has got rid of the luminous black and red.

But we still have tonight to dread.

Emily Beck (11)
Highfields Primary School, Burntwood

World War

W ar is the symbol of death every day,
O n some days there is a blanket where the dead lay,
R ifles firing bullets every day,
L onely families didn't think it was fair,
D eath was everywhere.

W ar is like an angry, evil bear,
A nd it doesn't want to stop killing,
R oaring and demolishing anything in its path
but it's not the last stage.

Brett Punnett (10)
Highfields Primary School, Burntwood

Creation Of The Four Seasons

Into quarters it's cut, like a birthday cake,
How clever was God, when He decided to make.
The flowers, colours, animals to grow,
He even made sun, moon, wind and snow.

Flowers rising from the soil,
The heat is hot, you're about to boil.
The blossom is rising from the trees,
The animals are coming like the bees.

There's a clear blue sky and a scorching sun,
It looks like I'm having fun.
There are blazing yellow flowers which feel so smooth,
So then I decided to move.
The scorching sun was burning,
As it decided to start turning.

There are frosty trees and frosty leaves,
But can we have some snow please?
The freezing cold,
And some people are bold.

Leanne Bennett (11)
Highfields Primary School, Burntwood

World War II

When every man went to the tragic place
One by one they died.
Rifles being loaded with extreme power,
Leaving families in pain and agony,
Dying in the cold, grey winds.
What should they do in the piercing winds
With crisp, chilly trees?
Aching, inflamed bombs dropping from German planes,
Running to shelter, to shelter.

Alyce Witton (10)
Highfields Primary School, Burntwood

The Volcano Is Like A Fire-Breathing Dragon

The volcano is like a fire-breathing dragon
Breathing fire and all it leaves is devastation.
It fires up high in the air,
It cools as it climbs down here and there.

It destroys everything in its path,
People who saw it wouldn't dare to laugh.
The lava is a deep, dark, deadly red,
It washes towns away leaving people dead.

It towers its body all over the town,
Then it dances and prances and jumps up and down.
Now it has destroyed the town,
Everyone there is wearing a frown.

When the long day has passed
The terrible eruption didn't last.
Now the eruption has suffocated the city,
Everything's ruined, what a pity.

Holly Goodwin-Wilcox (9)
Highfields Primary School, Burntwood

Happiness Poem

Happiness is like a bird flying in the sky.
Happiness is kind and truthful, it can never die.
Happiness is yellow like the golden sunshine.
Happiness is really sweet, it's the power divine.
Happiness sounds like joy and love throughout the land,
It overcomes sadness and buries it in sand.
Happiness tastes like chocolate, milk and cream.
Happiness is lovely, it is like a dream.
Happiness smells like cookies baked in an oven.
Happiness will stay forever, it is God's burden.
Happiness feels like true love's gift,
Some people help you by giving you a lift,
For happiness reminds you of the joy in man,
It is God's gift for all the land.

Scott Waldron (9)
Highfields Primary School, Burntwood

Seasons Change!

Try to wrap up warm
Or get frostbite on your toes,
Playing in the snow all day
As ice on water grows.

The spring blossom on the trees fall
And some trees are waiting bare,
Lambs are playing in the field,
Aromas float through the air.

The summer blossom transforms
Into vibrant, scented, emerald leaves,
The scent of the brightly coloured roses
Is enough to make you sneeze.

The bronzed autumn leaves crunch up,
The bark discolours on the rough trees,
Squirrels play amongst rustic pillows
As a cold current sways in the breeze.

Stacey Ruttenberg (11)
Highfields Primary School, Burntwood

Happiness

H appiness is yellow like the flowers in the field.
A rose for happiness to be my shield
P lants that smell like perfume so sweet.
P eople have happiness in their hearts so neat.
I n their hearts it's just like love,
N ever seeing a happy dove.
E veryone likes happiness, even I do.
S ome other people like it too,
S o let's have happiness and enjoy our lives.

Kate Hanmer (9)
Highfields Primary School, Burntwood

A Rainfall Is Dribbling Teardrops

Rainfall is like dribbling teardrops,
Into the muddy puddle it plops.

As it smashes on the ground
It gives a sort of sprinkling sound.

Water is all you can see
As it splashes gently all over me.

You see the anger in its eyes
As it shadows against the dark, gloomy skies.

As your hand wipes over your nose,
Stopping the teardrop dampening your clothes.

As it trickles down the drain
The tears run down the windowpane.

It splashes down onto the street
And on all the people I care to meet.

However, on calmer nights in May,
Whatever word you say . . .

Echoes in the moonlight.

Katie Gough (10)
Highfields Primary School, Burntwood

Happiness

Happiness is yellow like the sun, high and blazing in the sky.
Happiness sounds like the birds and bees buzzing and chirping away.
Happiness tastes like melted chocolate in marshmallows still hot.
Happiness looks like a baby lamb skipping away.
Happiness feels like a child happy and smiling in their glowing face.
Happiness reminds me of a flower just opened.

Amber Howe (11)
Highfields Primary School, Burntwood

The Big Wave

People running everywhere,
A tidal wave here and there,
People sleeping in their beds
While a tidal wave rushed through their head.

Tidal wave was really bad,
The people were so sad,
Some people survived,
Most of them died.

Most of the people were drowned,
People were begging on the ground,
There was a mess all around,
People buried in the ground.

Lots of people lost their things,
We are giving away our things,
People's houses were washed away,
The tidal wave happened on Boxing Day.

Lee Connock (10)
Highfields Primary School, Burntwood

Love

Love is pink, as pink as a soft subtle rose.
Love sounds like doves hovering in the sky.
Love is so sweet like a ripe, juicy strawberry.
Love smells like delicious, elegant perfume.
Love feels like silky petals off a rose.
Love looks like butterflies flapping in the sky.
Love reminds me of a swing swaying in the moonlight
And sparkling stars up above.

Aimee Wood (9)
Highfields Primary School, Burntwood

Eagles Are Hovering Birds

Eagles are hovering birds
Looking around for prey.
Claws as sharp as carving knives,
They take people's lives.

A sharp beak
As it scarily flaps its wings over the tallest peak.
Wings made of feathers,
As velvety as heathers.

As midday draws near
All you can hear
Is destruction and madness
And cries of sadness.

As the sun dies down
The eagle rests
In its nest.
The animals have tried their best
To pass its test.

Jamie Thorpe (10)
Highfields Primary School, Burntwood

Happiness Poem

Happiness is yellow like the great shiny sun.
Happiness sounds like birds singing beautifully in a big oak tree.
Happiness tastes like a juicy, refreshing orange.
Happiness smells like a bottle of new perfume which is sweet.
Happiness looks like buttercups and daises grouped together,
Moving slowly in the gentle breeze.
Happiness feels like an old teddy bear which you cuddle at night.
Happiness reminds me of the sand by the sea with beautiful
Patterns marked by the people who were there before.

Lauren Craik (10)
Highfields Primary School, Burntwood

World War II

All you see is exploding bombs
Scattering blood all around,
Hopeful people singing love songs,
At the same time crying their eyes out,
Children looking for their mums.
Suddenly guns shooting your way,
'Help me!' people cry.
I'm hungry and scared but yet still hopeful,
Before the war children screaming in happiness
But now they're screaming for their lives.
Hitler is the main criteria,
Peaceful night, sunny days, happy lives before the war,
But now just gone, happy days just gone,
Now all you see is smoke and hate,
We need You Lord.

Nathaniel Schofield (10)
Highfields Primary School, Burntwood

The Thailand Disaster

There was an earthquake under the sea
When people were holidaying happily,
The wave sounded like thunder,
What's that noise? the people wonder.

They look around, they start screaming,
The wave is shining, almost gleaming,
Eating everything in its way,
Nothing left the following day.

People clinging on to trees,
Trembling from their knees.
It all happened on Boxing Day,
People dead, running away.

We give money to help them survive,
So lots of people stay alive.

Emma Allwood (10)
Highfields Primary School, Burntwood

War

Bombs are dropping from the planes,
Burning and smashing on the ground.
People screaming and shouting for their lives,
Houses burning in the dark sky.

You can hear planes and the piercing noise
Of the air raid siren.
Food is getting rationed,
Children play but then need to get to air raid shelters.

Aaron Bishton (9)
Highfields Primary School, Burntwood

Emotions Poem

Anger is red like a petal of a rose,
Anger sound like a whistle blowing through your nose.
Anger tastes like a lot of steam,
Anger smells like a person long away from a dream.
Anger looks like a really big tomato,
Anger reminds me of a red-hot chilli pepper.

Chris Bullock (9)
Highfields Primary School, Burntwood

Love

Love is pink, as pink as a heart,
It sounds like roses swaying in the dark,
A moon from me to you in the moonlight dark,
It tastes like a ripe, gorgeous strawberry.

Love smells like fresh roses.
Love looks like a heart in the sky.
Love feels like butterflies in the sky.

Samantha Price (10)
Highfields Primary School, Burntwood

The Soldiers Of World War II

The 11th of the 11th we all remember,
Such a significant month as November,
Two minutes at the beginning of the day,
As we sit there and think, waiting to pray.

Soldiers alone, fighting, uncared,
Families at home frightened and scared.

Just imagine if you had to fight
And do without sleep all through the night,
When things go bang and bombs go off
And you catch that dreadful chesty cough.

Soldiers alone, fighting, uncared,
Families at home frightened and scared.

You fight for your life and then you get shot,
You remember your families and get all hot,
You steady yourself - you need a hand,
But feebly you fall to the sand.

Soldiers alone, fighting, uncared,
Families at home frightened and scared.

We must always think and remember,
Especially in the month of November,
We wear poppies that are red, black and green,
Everyone wears one, even the Queen.

Soldiers alone, fighting, uncared,
Families at home frightened and scared.

All they have is two minutes silence
To remember them as they fought in violence,
Bloodshed and death was told to cease
And thanks to the soldiers we now live in peace.

Soldiers alone, fighting, uncared,
Families at home frightened and scared.

Charlotte Goodwin-Wilcox (11)
Highfields Primary School, Burntwood

World War II

Bombs are falling through the air,
The running sound like a roaring bear,
The air raid siren making tears,
Waking up our darkest fears.

War is dangerous, battling deathly,
Fighting, scary and upsetting,
Children crying, people dying,
Don't know why they're crying or dying.

Bombs are dropping from the plane,
The shrapnel smashing on the windowpane.
The soldiers running really fast,
The tanks driving past.

Jessica Lloyd (10)
Highfields Primary School, Burntwood

What Does Christmas Mean?

What does Christmas mean to me?
It means
Friendship,
Family,
Love
And presents.

What does Christmas mean to other people?
It means
Christmas trees,
Baubles,
Love,
Family
And presents.

What does Christmas mean to poor people?
A cardboard box
On a cold wet floor!

Kyle Brannagan (10)
Howes Primary School, Coventry

Castle Vampire

The big iron door
Crashes as it shuts.
There is blood on the floor,
Cobwebs hang on the ceiling.

It is icy cold,
Sends a shiver down my spine.
The window slams
As the wind pounds hard.

Something hits my shoulder,
I look round.
No one is there.
Why did I do this stupid dare?

Out came Dracula
With his sharp teeth.
Blood on his chin,
'Ah! something to eat!'

I ran down the stairs
And out of the door.
My heartbeat racing,
Not going in there anymore!

Lauren Bowell (10)
Howes Primary School, Coventry

Rainbow

Rainbows are shiny and wonderful,
They stretch across the sky,
Pink, blue and yellow,
Maybe more colours next time.

The rain has all dried up.
The sun shines hot and strong.
Blue's the only colour you see,
Maybe more next time in the sky.

Amil Rehman (11)
Howes Primary School, Coventry

No Winners - Just Losers!

It was Christmas morning
Cold and fair
When the gangs crept out
Into the air.

There were two gangs
White and black
And they started to fight
Back to back.

The white gang lost
And fled as they could
By the icy river
They were trapped and stood.

Now the leaders
They came to the fore
They pushed and teased
Each other more.

One from each side
Stood and fought
Clawing and spitting
To be the winner they sought.

Punch for punch
Kick for kick
They fell into the river
Rushing and thick.

Then clinging together
Holding tight
They struggled so hard
Not to give up the fight.

The river took over, no strength to keep trying
The gangs on the bank, watched helpless and crying.

Charlotte Wells-Mawdsley (10)
Howes Primary School, Coventry

The Trouble With My Brother

The trouble with my brother is that he's gone completely mad,
He smiles all the time, he is never ever sad.

He has started to chase chickens. He thinks they're cake,
But he goes completely mental when he has tender steak.

He thinks he is a dog, chasing the sheep on the farm,
But he really needs a doctor, to help him keep calm.

We took him to the doctors. He held onto the door.
He didn't want to go but we said it was the law.

He let go eventually but he still did scream,
The doctor prescribed him, some anti-mental cream.

When we put it on him, it only made it worse,
He turned into a lion, as though he had a curse.

We called the doctor again; he came round instantly.
We had biscuits and discussed it over tea.

He then ate the doctor. Head . . . to . . . foot!
Now he's locked up in a wooden hut.

Now we can't do anything about it,
He's moved from the hut to a cage.
But now he's even worse
And it's sent him in a rage.
Roar!

Kye Mills (11)
Howes Primary School, Coventry

My Best Friend

My best friend
Has lovely brown hair.
When we play games
She is always fair.
She has quite a funny laugh
And is very, very daft.

My best friend,
Her favourite colour is pink.
She has lots of jewellery
With silver links.

My best friend
She loves to swim.
She once swam
With a dolphin.

Tia Dhaliwal (11)
Howes Primary School, Coventry

Ice Cream

The ice cream man
He pulls the handle
And an avalanche of ice cream
Forms into a mountain
Resting on a wafer cone.

He picks up a bottle
And squeezes
A river of red blood
Onto the mountain
Of ice cream.

As he stabs in the chocolate stick
I stare.

James Carter (10)
Howes Primary School, Coventry

Dancing

Hip, hop,
Freestyle,
Modern too,
These are the dances
I love to do.

Gymnastics,
Jazz,
Swing dance too,
These are the dances
I love to do.

Tap,
Ballet,
Cheerleading too,
These are the dances
I love to do.

Lauren Keeling (10)
Howes Primary School, Coventry

Kelly Holmes

Running for Great Britain,
Kelly Holmes a star,
Winning gold medals,
The best by far,
Rapid runner,
Eager too!
Kelly Holmes
I support you!
Olympic champion,
Elegance with grace,
Speeding round the track,
Gold medal place.

Shannon O'Neill (11)
Howes Primary School, Coventry

Floppy The Rabbit

Floppy the rabbit is the fastest in the world,
If you pick him up he's the cutest in the world.

If you stroke him he'll bite,
If you try to take his food he's alright.

He's always burrowing
And he's always scurrying.
If you don't keep a eye on him
He'll jump in the bin.

He doesn't really come inside
but one day he realised
He can always pop in for a bite to eat.

He comes to the doorstep
Just to have a look,
If you let him in
He'll start looking for his tin.

One day he'll realise
That he can always
Pop in for tea.

Ellis Branski (11)
Howes Primary School, Coventry

My Dad!

My dad is cool,
He sometimes drives me to school.
My dad is weird,
He doesn't have a beard.
When I am sad he is always there,
When I am hurt he really does care.
He is very cheerful,
Not very tearful.
He is the best,
Better than all the rest.

Manisha Bhairon (10)
Howes Primary School, Coventry

Thriller

Blood on the tiles in the haunted house,
Eerie atmosphere demanding oxygen,
Stagger up the creepy steps.

See Dracula's coffin and Frankenstein's lair,
Hear the chattering teeth of a skeleton,
Gaze at flesh-eating zombies.

Race from Professor Zmad,
Dare to go to the monster's toilet,
Go up to the attic.

Step to the window,
Discover something scary,
You faint but do not wake.

For though you fight to stay alive the thriller has you.
Ha! Ha! Ha! Ha! Ha! Ha! Ha!

Adam Ellix (11)
Howes Primary School, Coventry

A Special Friend

A special friend makes me feel happy
When I am down.
I know I have found a new special friend,
She's funny, she's pretty, she's kind, she's cool.

When she's over my home
She likes telling secrets,
She always keeps them,
She is wicked to me.

That's why a special friend like Steph
Will always be my best friend.

She makes funny faces
And makes me laugh in class.

Kelly Moore (10)
Howes Primary School, Coventry

My Sister!

My sister is a show-off,
She thinks she is the best,
She pushes me and hurts me,
She really is a pest!

My sister is so noisy,
She snores while she's sleeping,
She has the biggest bedroom,
Downstairs you hear her leaping!

My sister is alright I guess,
Sometimes she is kind,
But maybe she's just acting
Or playing with my mind!

Ellie Takhar (10)
Howes Primary School, Coventry

A & N Rockers

I wanna rock, rock, rock when the sun goes down,
Ooh, ooh, ooh, ooh.
I wanna care, care, care when the moon glows up,
Ooh, ooh.
I wanna sing, sing, sing when the disco lights flash,
Ooh, ooh.
I wanna dance, dance, dance when the stars flash high,
Ooh, ooh, ooh, ooh.
I wanna shout, shout, shout when the rock bands play,
Ooh, ooh, ooh, ooh.
I wanna eat, eat, eat when the restaurants serve,
Ooh, ooh, ooh, ooh.
It's disco time and it's fun!
Ooh, ooh, ooh, ooh,
Ooh, ooh, ooh, ooh!

Abida Hasan (8)
Nelson Mandela School, Sparkbrook

My Eid Day

It was on my Eid day,
When the day started,
Stars were twinkling, twinkling
Shiny and bright.
And then the full moon appeared,
It was beautiful,
Because it was Eid, lovely and sweet!

All that food was shared out
And all the presents were shared out,
Because it was Eid, lovely and sweet!

And later that afternoon
When everybody gathered together
And they were wishing people,
Wishing people a happy Eid,
It was so wonderful,
Because it was Eid, lovely and sweet!

All that food was shared out
And all the presents were shared out,
Because it was Eid, lovely and sweet.

Anisha Hoque (10)
Nelson Mandela School, Sparkbrook

Rashurd's Cricket Dreams

It's England Vs West Indies,
England need six runs to win.
G Jones, Trescothick and K Ali have tried their best
But no luck.
Here comes Rashurd he's on the pitch
And here we go,
He hits it . . . si . . . si . . . si . . . six,
Six all the way!

Rashurd Umar Ali (9)
Nelson Mandela School, Sparkbrook

Family Food

I like pizza with loads of cheese,
My sister likes pizza with a few peas,
My mummy likes pizza on the phone,
My daddy likes pizza when he's home alone.

I like pasta with loads of sauce,
My sister likes pasta when she sits on a horse,
My mummy likes pasta when it's from home,
My daddy likes pasta but he moans and groans.

I like apples when I'm in bed,
My sister likes apples when they're shiny red,
My mummy likes apples when she's on a cliff,
My daddy likes apples but only Granny Smith.

I like fish fingers nice and hot,
My sister likes fish fingers in a blue pot,
My mummy likes fish fingers squidgy and flat,
My daddy likes fish fingers shaped as a bat.

I like bananas nice and cream,
My sister likes bananas with a tangerine,
My mummy likes bananas with a pinch of salt,
My daddy likes bananas on a big blue boat.

Hassan Sharif (7)
Nelson Mandela School, Sparkbrook

New Shoes

My shoes are new and squeaky shoes,
They're shiny, creaky shoes,
I wish I had my leaky shoes
That my mother threw away.

I liked my old brown, leaky shoes
Much better than these creaky shoes,
These shiny, creaky, squeaky shoes
I got to wear today.

Shajhon Miah (9)
Nelson Mandela School, Sparkbrook

Sun

What I like about the sun
Is when it shines on me.

What I hate about the sun
Is when it shines in my eyes.

What I like about the sun
Is when it goes around in the sky.

What I hate about the sun
Is when it doesn't shine.

What I like about the sun
Is when we can play out in the sun.

What I hate about the sun
Is when we get too hot and thirsty.

Hamza Latif (7)
Nelson Mandela School, Sparkbrook

Like And Hate

What I like about lightning
Is when it frightens my cousin out of my room.

What I hate about lightning
Is when it makes a big hole in the roof.

What I like about lightning
Is when my mum is telling me off,
She worries about the lightning instead of telling me off!

What I hate about lightning
Is when it hurts other people.

What I like about lightning
Is when it makes big noises.

Jordan McIntosh (7)
Nelson Mandela School, Sparkbrook

Weather - Like And Hate

What I like about the overcast sun
It is hot and breezy, mildly.

What I hate about the overcast sun
Is when the clouds shimmer away swiftly.

What I like about the sun
Is when it shines on me, bright and light.

What I hate about the sun
Is when it disappears.

What I hate about the rain
Is when it drips and drops slowly.

What I like about the rain
Is when it only splashes on me quickly.

What I hate about the wind
Is when it makes my hair messy angrily.

What I like about the wind
Is when it blows me away quickly.

What I hate about the lightning
Is how it kills people painfully.

What I like about the lightning
Is how it makes different colours in the sky gently.

Karina Kaur (8)
Nelson Mandela School, Sparkbrook

Like And Hate

What I like about the rain
Is when I get wet happily.

What I hate about the rain
Is that I can't ride my bike frustratingly.

What I like about the sun
Is that I can play on my bouncy castle joyfully.

What I hate about the sun
Is when I have to put on suncream glumly.

What I like about the wind
Is the sound it makes loudly.

What I hate about the wind
Is when it makes you cold and chilly.

What I like about the lightning
Is when it flashes brightly.

What I hate about the lightning
Is when it makes people die painfully.

What I like about the snow
Is because I can have snowball fights gleefully.

What I hate about the snow
Is when it melts away slowly.

Krishan Lawrence (8)
Nelson Mandela School, Sparkbrook

Sun

What I like about the sun
Is when it makes me sweaty.

What I hate about the sun
Is when it shines in my eyes.

What I like about the sun
Is when I play outside with my friends.

What I hate about the sun
Is when it makes me too hot.

What I like about the sun
Is when I sit outside in the garden.

What I hate about the sun
Is when it's too bright.

Abdallah Warsame (7)
Nelson Mandela School, Sparkbrook

Snow

What I like about the snow
Is when I can have snow fights.

What I hate about the snow
Is when my hands and ears get freezing cold.

What I like about the snow
Is when I can make a snowman.

What I hate about the snow
Is when snowflakes go on my body and make me shiver.

What I like about the snow
Is when the school is closed. Hooray!

What I hate about the snow
Is when the snow blizzard hits my face.

Obaid Mohammed (8)
Nelson Mandela School, Sparkbrook

Flutter, Flutter

Flutter, flutter
What colour are you?

Flutter, flutter
You smell like roses?

Flutter, flutter,
Fly so bright.

Flutter, flutter
Flash at night.

Flutter, flutter
Sit on a rose.

Flutter, flutter
Say goodnight
But don't forget
To say goodbye.

Wait on flutter, flutter
Please don't go,
If you go one day
I will be kind
And you'll have to
Listen to me!

Akeel Malik (8)
Nelson Mandela School, Sparkbrook

Tauseef's Cricket Dreams

There's a match against Pakistan - it's Australia.
Wasim Akhtar takes a shot and it's a catch and that's *out!*
Inzamam-ul-Haq holds his bat high and takes a great shot
And oh not it's a catch and that's the end,
We won't be seeing him for the rest of the game.
Here comes M Tauseef Latif and it's 1 ball and 5 runs to win,
Can Tauseef make it?
M Tauseef Latif takes a sweep and, and, and *it's a big six*
And Tauseef wins the game for Pakistan once again.

Tauseef Latif (9)
Nelson Mandela School, Sparkbrook

Summer Fun

Sunshine,
All is fine,
In car,
Not far,
Park 'n' ride,
Seaside,
On sand,
As planned,
Deckchairs,
Take care,
Swimwear,
Somewhere,
Don't howl,
Lost towel,
Beach clad,
Even Dad,
Beach skin,
Water skim,
One splash,
All dash,
One shout,
All out,
Soaking wet,
No regret,
Water salty,
Not my fault-y,
Awful thirst,
Drink first,
Beach flop,
Lollipop,
Hot feet,
Lunch eat,
Mum burns,
Body turns,
Dad snores,
Both bores,
Sand play,
Hooray!

Real hassle,
Sandcastle,
Bat, ball,
Sister call,
Run, catch,
No match,
Getting late,
Bus waits,
Goodbye,
Sea, sky,
Summer fun,
Number one.

Alishah Hussain (7)
Nelson Mandela School, Sparkbrook

The Haunted House

Step in through the rusty gates,
Be as quiet as a mouse.
We're going to sneak and take a peek inside the haunted house.

Vampires get ready,
Ghastly ghouls lurk on the stairs,
Imps and sprites have pillow fights to catch you unawares.

Wizards in the kitchen make slug and spider pies,
Vampires complete a maths test,
All the spooks must look their best!

Moving dolls,
Put lipstick on.
Hurray, to the Spooks Ball,
Then morning will be here anon.

Run, run as fast as you can,
Be silent as a mouse.
Tiptoe out while you still can,
Escape the haunted house!

Nosheen Mahmood (8)
Nelson Mandela School, Sparkbrook

Fred The Cat

I am a black cat,
My name is Fred.
I live next door
To my best friend Ted.
I'm not that fat,
I'm not that thin,
I have a two day meal,
But I'm still a pin.
I don't have a mum,
I don't have a dad,
In fact I have a landlord
Who is really mad.
I have two ears,
Also fluffy fur
And a small, little mouth
To do a gentle purr.
I wake up at six,
Eat at nine,
Relax at four,
At six I dine.
I'm really happy,
I'm really calm
And when I'm tired . . .
I stay at a farm.
I help others
When I'm free,
Or else . . .
I play with Lee.
I'm an old cat
And my name's Fred!

Sidrah Mahmood (11)
Nelson Mandela School, Sparkbrook

Why War? Why War?

Why is war the answer?
Slowly go to war,
End is near go through the door,
War is the end to life.

Why war? Why war?
It does no good at all,
Only leaves us . . . dead!

Why is war the answer?
Rain pelting on your head,
There is a chance you will be dead,
War is the end to life.

Why war? Why war?
It does no good at all,
Only leaves us . . . dead!

Why is war the answer?
Everybody fighting true,
People running quickly, hiding,
War is the end to life.

Why war? Why war?
It does no good at all,
Only leaves us . . . dead!

Why is war the answer?
Battlefield cries,
Everybody dies,
War is the end to life.

Why war? Why war?
It does no good at all,
Only leaves us . . . dead!

Jordan Edgar (10)
Newdigate Primary School, Bedworth

Tsunami

My eyes didn't believe what I saw,
My heart ripped up and tore,
The wave crashing over me,
I quickly ran out of the sea,
Why did this happen God?

Now I'm sad and all alone,
Not even with a little home,
I think this happened for a reason,
I really hated the Christmas season,
Why did this happen God?

My parents have gone away
And I have nowhere yet to stay,
At night I feel my heart beating,
Feelings are overheating,
Why did this happen God?

Now I'm sad and all alone,
Not even with a little home,
I think this happened for a reason,
I hated the Christmas season,
Why did this happen God?

Zoe Harrison (11)
Newdigate Primary School, Bedworth

An Ode To My Mum!

Her eyes shine like glittering stars,
She's got the nicest heart by far,
Her lips are as red as a rose,
Just like her shimmering toes.

She keeps me safe,
Because she is very brave,
She was there for me when I was young,
The cuddles and the kisses all year long.
An ode to my mum.

Zoe Keers (11)
Newdigate Primary School, Bedworth

Tsunami!

As I saw the wave come crashing,
All I saw was almighty flashing,
Now I feel really sad,
Everyone is running round mad,
I wish it'd never happened!

I've lost everything and my home
And now I'm all alone,
Now the wave has gone crashing through,
Everything is so not true,
I wish it'd never happened!

Now I've got no family,
How can I live happily?
Families are now dead, yes it's true,
As the tsunami fled through and through
I wish it'd never happened!

Lauren Lessels (10)
Newdigate Primary School, Bedworth

Ode To My Mum

Her eyes shone upon the light,
Her face twinkled through the night.
She's always smiling like the sun
And helping me until I've done.

Mum's shine beats a dull, dull day,
Her love I don't have to pay.
She's as sweet as a red, red rose,
She's never in a deep, deep doze.

She talks to me when I am down,
Then I never have to frown.
She's as sweet as a candy cane,
Her love I don't have to gain.

Gaby Fox (11)
Newdigate Primary School, Bedworth

Dreams

All of my dreams are really strange,
Some I wish that I could change,
When I fall asleep at night,
I may get a little fright.

In my dreams I dream
Of wigs made of whipped cream,
Hamsters that are bright blue,
Even falling down the loo,
My dreams are really mad.

Like a ghost is now my dad,
But it doesn't make me sad,
When my cousin couldn't speak,
In my dreams he had a beak,
But my dreams never come true.

Sometimes I go to Mars
And I drive in a mega big car,
Then I go to the moon,
Then I buy ten yellow spoons,
Then I come back to Earth.

Finally I wake up quickly,
Sit up and take a look around,
My dreams are now not so real.

Chelsee Mckinley (11)
Newdigate Primary School, Bedworth

An Ode To Mother

A mother's love
Is like a rose,
Every day
It grows and grows.

Except when you
Get sent to bed,
Then the rose
Turns angry red.

Forgiveness and
A key to heart,
A finish and
A lovely start.

Does it matter,
Pink rose, white?
With her there's
A shining light.

The rose is big,
The thorn is small
But the petals
Will one day, fall.

Ellie Gough (10)
Newdigate Primary School, Bedworth

War!

I hear the trigger of the gun,
I hear the soldiers cry and run,
Some of the soldiers get wounded and die,
We look out and see them lie,
When will this end?

All of the bombs drive me round the bend,
When is this terror going to end?
Wives will cry
When they see them lie,
When will this end?

I hear the trigger of the gun,
I hear the soldiers cry and run,
Some of the soldiers get wounded and die,
We look out and see them lie,
When will this end?

Leigh Cooke (10)
Newdigate Primary School, Bedworth

An Ode To My Nan

My love for her will always be strong,
No matter what she does, right or wrong,
She's always calm like a sunny day,
I wouldn't like her another way.

She's been there for me day by day,
We go for walks in the mornings of May,
Her love for me will never end,
She always there, my special friend.

If she ever goes away,
Her love stays in my heart every day,
I know for sure she loves me so,
Her love in my heart will never go.

Ruby Hallam (11)
Newdigate Primary School, Bedworth

Why?

Why is this happening?
How long will it take for help to arrive?
When will people start rebuilding their lives?
Who did this?
What help will people get?
Where will this happen next?
How many people will survive?

Why are people's lives being destroyed?
How long will this last?
Who has survived the tsunami?
Where are the children's parents?
When will this pain ever end?
How is help getting there?
Who will help?
Show you care.

Leah Paxton (11)
Newdigate Primary School, Bedworth

An Ode To My Dog

His coat shines like a golden stone,
His eyes twinkle when he gets a bone,
His love is so very nice,
He will not even eat real mice.

He shows his love by licking me,
His cuddles are so nice you'll see,
When I give him loads of food,
He'll hide it if he's in a mood.

He's only three,
But he still loves me.

Jessica Shortall (10)
Newdigate Primary School, Bedworth

Ode To My Puppy Milly

Your eyes shine in the night,
They even shine in the light,
You like to run around the park,
You get on my nerves when you start to bark.

Your fur is like silky sheets,
You play with everyone that you meet,
Your heart is like a golden star,
You like to go in my car.

I love you so very much,
You like to be fussed and touched,
You always keep me very safe
And you love to stuff your face.

Alyshea Ingram (10)
Newdigate Primary School, Bedworth

Untitled

War, war, war,
People came with all their might,
War is wrong,
But they came to fight.

Cry, cry, cry,
Cry your eyes out,
Be afraid of what just happened,
Just cry silently for those who died.

Sad, sad, sad,
You made me upset,
It isn't a joke,
Haven't we peace yet?

Cherise Johnson (10)
Newdigate Primary School, Bedworth

Ode To My Grandma

Her eyes shine like a star in the sky,
Her teeth twinkle when she passes by,
Her heart is a ruby shining bright
And she is lovely in daylight.

She shows her love by spoiling me,
So she is the best grandma you will see,
When I need her she makes sure I'm safe,
In God she has got a lot of faith.

I love her very much,
When we stay in touch,
I love you Grandma!

Leanne Redpath (10)
Newdigate Primary School, Bedworth

Across The Rainbow

Across the rainbow there could be
A happy place just waiting for me.
A bowl of ice cream,
A beach full of sand,
This would be ever so grand.
Bacon and eggs every morning,
Never up early
So there would be no yawning.
A path of rubies,
A table of wood,
If anyone could live here a fairy could.
A big green forest,
A castle,
A florist,
Now if you stop and take a think
What colour would the sky be?
Red, orange, black, blue or pink?

Abigail Ball (10)
St Andrew's CE Primary School, Weston

The Best Thing In The World

The best thing in the world to me
Isn't the golden honey from a bee.
It isn't the money being placed in my hand,
Or the gentle sea, nor the sun-warmed sand.
It isn't a cool, blanket of floating mist,
Or a stormy bay, angry and sunkissed.

The best thing in the world to you
Might be a cow's happy but low moo.
It might be a light showing you the way,
Or it could be the beginning and end of the day.
Maybe it's a flower growing from a bud,
Or it could be your life going as it should.

The best thing in the world to me
Doesn't cause any strain,
Or any pain.
It just makes me feel
Like I've got a good deal.
I don't care if I have to walk forever or eat a bug,
Because all that I want, is a hug!

Rosanna Churchill (11)
St Andrew's CE Primary School, Weston

Shopping!

I do love going shopping,
It is a pleasant treat.
My supermarket journey
Brings back more than I can eat!

A chicken, some lamb and lemonade too,
Jam and honey and a bit of vindaloo.
Chocolate and ice cream,
Steam pudding brimming with steam.
A pie or two, a joint of beef,
That really smells, good grief!

Ben Nadin (11)
St Andrew's CE Primary School, Weston

Monsters

Monsters come out at night
When there's nobody in sight.
They come in all different shapes and sizes
And they are full of nasty surprises.
They love flesh
And even eat dirty mess.
Some of them even have special powers,
Some of them even have showers.
They don't like the sun
But my goodness can they run!
Some are green, some are red,
Some have even got a thousand eyes in their head.
Some have claws,
Some have got very loud roars.
They even eat children like yours.

Blaine Pavlovic (9)
St Andrew's CE Primary School, Weston

Friends, Friends

Friends, friends they're really kind to me
And hopefully they always will be.
Laugh, laugh all day long,
Never doing anything wrong.
Sometimes meeting after school,
That is really, really cool.

Friends, friends great to be with,
I really love the life I live.
Zzzz, zzzz having sleepovers all the time,
There's nothing wrong with my friends,
They're all fine!

Emily Williams (11)
St Andrew's CE Primary School, Weston

They Are Here, They Won't Be For Long!

Bang! A gunshot sounds,
A black and white animal falls to the ground,
Grey orphans drop pearls of sorrow,
It will have no mother tomorrow,
A black furry animal will no longer roam,
Soon mankind will be alone,
The giant mammal in the sea
Will leave a gap for every eye to see,
A spotted carnivore there will no longer be,
With one shot it will be gone eternally,
Slithering around in every condition,
It will be gone from just one mission,
All these animals soon will be yesterday,
Stop it now is what they pray!

Lizzie Edgecombe (11)
St Andrew's CE Primary School, Weston

A Serious Letter To The Prime Minister

I know you are a busy man
But I am busy too
And I think it's time this matter
Was brought into your view.
There is a blotch on your society,
A stain that's like no other.
The species that I speak of
Is of course the little brother.
I now propose a law to you,
I'm sure you'll understand
To destroy all pesky little brothers
Right across the land!

Connor Moylett (10)
St Andrew's CE Primary School, Weston

The Clock

Tick . . . tock . . . tick . . . tock . . .
His eyes were magnetised to the hands of the clock.
Tick . . . tock . . . tick . . . tock . . .
The power it held wasn't easy to block.
Tick . . . tock . . . tick . . . tock . . .
The suspense in the room was uneasy to bear
But all of the room was involved in a stare.
Tick . . . tock . . . tick . . . tock . . .
The minute hand pushing its way to the top,
Going so slowly, please, please don't stop.
Tick . . . tock . . . tick . . . tock . . .
Finally, at last, as the hand points to the sky,
It's home time now!
School's finished.
Goodbye.

Torben Schwartz (11)
St Andrew's CE Primary School, Weston

Eat Your Greens

My dad always tells me to eat my greens,
I just say, 'No!'
He just says, 'Why?'
I just make up excuses.
He always tells me they will make me strong,
I used to believe him
But the other day in PE I wasn't that strong,
So I tried to give them to the dog,
But the dog just brought it back up.
I wish there never was such a thing as greens.
My dad said to me, 'Why can't you be like the rest?
And *eat your greens!*'
The compromise that we have reached
Is that I'll eat baked beans!

Becky Sallis (10)
St Andrew's CE Primary School, Weston

If It Were Up To Me!

If it were up to me
Elbows would be allowed on the table,
Please and thank yous would not be invented
And I could always eat with my mouth open!

If it were up to me
School would be history,
Maths would be for geeks
And school dinners would be thrown in the trash!

If it were up to me
Vegetables would be replaced with sweets,
Chocolate would be our main course
And trees of crisps and lollies would grow!

If it were up to me
My pocket money would be a lot more
Than just 50p,
Notes would fall from the sky!

If it were up to me
Dragons would roam the land,
Fairies would lend a helping hand,
Trolls would sleep under bridges!

And I would be the ruler of the world!

Alice Clifford (11)
St Andrew's CE Primary School, Weston

Going On And On . . .

Teacher's voice is droning on,
Concentration been and gone.
Blackboard's fading out of sight,
She won't notice . . . well, she might.
Slightly drooling, eyes grey and dull,
I'm standing on a giant ship's hull!
The sea is rolling, I feel quite ill,
I'm lying on the greenest hill.
The sun is shining, burning my skin,
I'm sitting in a rubbish bin!
The stench is unearthly, I need to get out!
I'm in a busy city, people scream and shout.
The whole world is here, or so it may seem,
I'm chilling by a peaceful stream.
The silence is interrupted by a roaring waterfall!
It's making such a din like an angry buzzard's call . . .
I bet that now you're thinking
Where will this poem end?
What planet is this author on?
When will she break the trend?
So I'll bring it to a closure,
I'll cut it nice and short.
I have a short attention span,
I just cannot be taught!

Charley Turton (10)
St Andrew's CE Primary School, Weston

Days Of The Week

Monday, Tuesday
Go away,
Wednesday, Thursday
You're here to stay.
Friday, Saturday
Seem a mile away,
Sunday here we go again,
Here is a week of pain.

Maths - timetable,
I'm really able.
English you're the best,
I don't like any of the rest.
One day has gone, another four to go,
Tomorrow science oh! Oh!
Science I don't like you,
Great the class is over, yahoo!
History is next, I'm walking to the class,
I get some homework, oh blast,
End of week has come,
Weekend has come oh yes, yes
This is the best.

Seena Boroomand (11)
St Andrew's CE Primary School, Weston

The Witch

The witch is horrible and tall.
She's hairy and ghastly.
Her face is rotting at the sides
Round her nose and her eyes.
The skin has been eaten by maggots.
She kills children all over the world.
She's a simply horrid sight.

Stephanie Horsley (7)
St Andrew's CE Primary School, Weston

Animals In The Jungle

A sweet little parrot perched on a tree,
A big yellow leopard staring at me.
A camouflaged chameleon I think I just saw,
Deep in the jungle the lions roar.
A tall giraffe dressed in spots,
His skin is like a decorated pot.
The monkeys drinking from the river,
As they lick it the water begins to shiver.
Then the monkeys eat their lunch,
Eating bananas by the bunch.
In the lakes full of fish,
Wild dogs not eating from a dish.
Elephants stomping on the ground,
Exciting animals to be found.
Now they have all gone to bed,
Ready for a busy day ahead.

Demi Douglas (10)
St Andrew's CE Primary School, Weston

The Sun

The sun, the sun is always shining,
The sun, the sun is never dull.
The sun sometimes hides,
The sun is mostly out.
The sun is like a fireball in the sky.
The sun is like something that would blind you.
The sun is like a red-hot fireball circling around the world.
The sun can make you peel.
The sun can make you turn brown,
But without the precious sun in the sky
We are sure to frown.

Luke Bradbury (11)
St Andrew's CE Primary School, Weston

The One And Only Meerkat

The liker of the luscious grass,
The owner of his territory,
The adorer of the shimmering sun,
The lover of powerful glory!

The admirer of the scorpions,
The villager living in flowers,
The noisy little creature
That has some unlikely powers!

The ability to scatter,
The king that loves to crunch,
The specialist on ranging,
The one who adores his lunch!

The talented searcher,
The treasure of the land,
The queen of the entire kingdom,
The unlikely man!

The wandering animal,
The incredible lover,
It could only be another . . .
Meerkat!

Charlotte Palmer-Hollinshead (10)
St Andrew's CE Primary School, Weston

My Best Friend, Saskia

M y best friend, Saskia,
Y elling out my name.

B est friends all our lives
E ating chocolate is our game.
S itting on the sofa watching TV
T ime is wasted.

F inding trouble everywhere,
R acing around the green,
I wish I was taller now.
E very day I play with her.
N ow in school she's in a different class
D arkness goes past her eyes as she sleeps.

S askia, Saskia, wake up.
A sleep on the sofa now we are
S leeping, sleeping, sleeping time away.
K nock, knock at the door.
I s it Saskia?
A n excellent friend she is to me.

Christina Allen (10)
St Andrew's CE Primary School, Weston

The Weather

When the sun comes out everybody screams and shouts.
When the rain falls down everyone just sits and frowns.
When autumn arrives all the leaves fall off the trees,
Happy as a dancing bee.
When winter is here the snow trickles down and covers the ground,
Anything that's under there will never be found.
I've just written about the weather and the seasons,
So I've also written about the world's reasons.

Amy Setterfield-Smith (10)
St Andrew's CE Primary School, Weston

Food

Custard, jelly, chocolate sauce,
All this food has made me hoarse.
Ice cream, cake, dripping honey,
Oohh I think I'm going to belch.
Aw I think I'm going to swell,
I think I'm on my way to Hell!
Food,
More food,
Even more food,
I can't cope
No more.
Need to belch,
Not on the floor,
Go and stand outside the door.
Belch, yuck!
Clean it up,
Oh no,
No more!

Matthew Barrett (10)
St Andrew's CE Primary School, Weston

Cats

Some are small, some are tall,
Some are even very cruel,
Some are fat, some are lean,
They're the ones who keep very clean,
Some are fluffy, some are spotty,
Some look cute and very dotty.

I wonder who my favourite will be?
Is it Burmese, Siamese, or Tonkinese?
I think it's probably Burmese,
Because she's part Siamese and looks Chinese,
But it doesn't really matter at all,
Because all cats are beautiful, crazy and cool!

Stephanie Golding (9)
St Anne's Catholic Primary School, Weeping Cross

On My Bike

Riding my bike through Cannock Chase
Speeding along through dirt tracks
With the wind in my face.

There was lots of mud and lumps
It was hard work to get to the top of the hill.
I got to the top
I had to stop.
Going down it was like I was flying
And it gave me a thrill.

At the bottom of the hill was a stream
And lots of mud,
Going through this made me feel good.

Chilled to the bone,
Time to go home.

James Lewis (10)
St Anne's Catholic Primary School, Weeping Cross

Suki

I always thought it would be cool and funky
If Mum would let me have a monkey.
I asked for one for my birthday,
But she looked at me and said, *'No way!'*

She said that I am monkey enough,
(I really thought she was being quite tough).
But in the end she bought me a cat,
And so I had to settle with that.

But Suki the cat is like a brother,
I wouldn't wish for anything other.
He often goes to the top of our tree,
He really is like a little monkey!

Amy-Rose Bayliffe (9)
St Anne's Catholic Primary School, Weeping Cross

My Day At Highbury

Woke up this morning,
feeling great,
we're going to Highbury,
don't want to be late.

Come on Dad,
let's get in the car,
the coach is from Molineux,
it's not far.

Sitting on the coach,
playing games,
having a raffle,
and guessing players' names.

Looking at the pitch,
the players come out,
they begin to warm up,
the supporters all shout.

It was a close first half,
and the score is 0-0,
so I get on the phone
to tell my brother Will.

In the second half
Wolves do well,
but all of a sudden,
in the penalty area Henry fell.

Viera then scored,
from the penalty spot,
but Wolves fought back
And Arsenal look the best - not.

Arsenal broke free,
as Wolves tried to score,
and Ljungberg had a shot,
to score one more.

With Wolves losing 2-0,
at the final whistle,
there was no way to beat Arsenal,
who were as sharp as a thistle.

Adam Haycox (9)
St Anne's Catholic Primary School, Weeping Cross

Golf-Keeper

Golf-keeper, that's what I want to be
But who is going to guide me
Because I'm uncertain you see
And what I finally become is really up to me

I love to play in goal
As football is really in my soul
Saving shots is what I do best
And makes me stand out from all the rest

Golf is my second sport
But yet again my scores support
Another opportunity for me to excel
And make a living at something I do well

I love to take part in both my chosen sports
And try my best at being the best
But when it comes down to what I do best
Who really cares because I can only try my best

The final decision on what I'll become
Lies in the future of an unknown outcome
But whatever it is
I'll always try to be the best I can be.

Dale Reaney (10)
St Anne's Catholic Primary School, Weeping Cross

My Dog

My dog is beautiful
He doesn't bite.
He's brown all over his body.
On his tummy he has a patch of white.

He runs around a lot,
He is very fast.
When I try to race him,
He just goes flying past.

He really doesn't like the cat,
I'll never understand why,
They always seem to have a fight,
The cat ends up jumping up high.

His name is Milo,
He runs to and fro.
He chases all the birds
Until they fly and go.

Jed Davies (10)
St Anne's Catholic Primary School, Weeping Cross

Chocolate

Chocolate is tasty, it makes a big mess,
Your mum always tells you to eat less.
White or dark, it doesn't matter,
But all the teachers say it will make you fatter!

I always eat it twice a day,
Once at lunch and once at play.
Eating it is a special treat,
It always, always smells so sweet!

A secret box of it under my bed,
I hope my brother doesn't get there instead,
Timeout and Dairy Milk Wafer,
Cadbury's are the best chocolate makers!

Caitlin Astbury (10)
St Anne's Catholic Primary School, Weeping Cross

Summer Holidays

In the summer holidays it's always sunny,
And it is rather funny,
Sitting licking ice cream,
Having a little daydream,
Plus there is no school for a while,
So I can do everything my style!

We go for a run
In the summer sun,
Which is a lot of fun.
It's not like wintry snow,
Stuck in scarves and hats with nowhere to go,
Because it's the *summer holidays.*

Bluebells and roses smell so sweet,
(Not like my dad's smelly feet).
I sit and make daisy chains,
Until autumn, when it starts to rain.
Rolling around the grass like a fool,
Not quite looking forward to . . .
Going back to school!

Kia Hunt (9)
St Anne's Catholic Primary School, Weeping Cross

What Makes Me Happy?

I am happy when I have a surprise,
I am happy when I eat chocolate,
I am happy when I see my friend,
I am happy when I do my homework,
I am happy when I go to school,
I am happy when I watch TV,
I am happy when my mum tells me a story,

But most of all, I will be happy when I see *God.*

Samantha Kalonji (10)
St Anne's Catholic Primary School, Weeping Cross

In The Playground

10.30 and the bell is ringing,
all the children come out singing.

Hopping, skipping, playing games,
shouting out each other's names.

Katie, Amy, Jade and Sue,
Laura, Jess and Chloe too.

Tag, catch and having fun,
outside playing in the sun.

Footballs shooting into goal,
what a save by big boy Joel.

Playtime ends as the whistle blows,
all line up and one line goes.

Back inside to learn some more,
Maths and English (what a bore).

Katie Harwood (9)
St Anne's Catholic Primary School, Weeping Cross

Seasons

The first season that comes up in the year is spring,
The flowers grow and Easter comes along.
Chocolate eggs are my favourite thing.

The next season is summer.
The sun comes out and school ends,
People going on holiday with their friends.

Then it is autumn,
When the leaves come down
And land softly on the ground.

Last of all is winter,
The coldest of them all,
When the snow starts to fall.

Hannah Powell (10)
St Anne's Catholic Primary School, Weeping Cross

I Love Food

I love food, food is great,
I eat everything, early or late.
Strange-shaped pasta, wibbly-wobbly jelly,
Multicoloured ice cream, all in my belly.

Big or small, hard or gooey,
I love food even if it's chewy.
At the table, on the floor,
Food tastes great, I always want more.

Sweet or savoury, spicy or mild,
I love everything and I'm only a child.
Think when I'm grown, all the foods I can eat,
I'll be so vast, I'll not see my feet.

I love food, food is great,
I eat everything, early or late.
I'd be so unhappy if there was no food,
I'm sure I'd always be in a horrible mood.

Sam Hogan-Cooper (10)
St Anne's Catholic Primary School, Weeping Cross

Seaside Fun

There were people having fun,
Running, swimming in the sun,
Children throwing pebbles in the sea
And grandparents eating a yummy cream tea.

Over the road in the sealife centre
There were flat fish, fat fish,
Swordfish, scary fish and a big sign saying,
Do not enter.

Children playing in the sand
Making sandcastles and burying Dad.
People going home with an ice cream in their hands,
Sand in their feet and sand in their toes,
And a great big blob of ice cream on their nose.

Jack Newport (10)
St Anne's Catholic Primary School, Weeping Cross

Holidays

I'm on my way to the beach,
I can see the golden sand,
There are lots of people sunbathing,
Sunbathing on the land.

The sea is sparkling blue,
Nearly as blue as the sky.
I can see the waves crashing,
But they don't crash too high.

My mum got me a hot dog
To eat there and then,
I couldn't finish it all,
So I gave it to Uncle Len.

The aeroplanes take-off,
Up, up they go,
They travel really, really fast,
But from the ground they look so slow.

I must put on my summer hat,
The sun is getting hot.
I can still see the aeroplane,
But now it's like a dot.

I think I'll go for a paddle
To cool my toes right down,
I've got white marks where my costume's been,
I think I'm going brown.

I'd better put my suncream on,
In case I start to burn.
There's a lady over there with bright red skin,
Some people never learn.

The holiday is over,
We are getting on the plane.
The sun has gone behind a cloud,
I think it's going to rain.

Katie Button (9)
St Anne's Catholic Primary School, Weeping Cross

Forest Fears

(Written after being on Cannock Chase with my family at night)

I saw the forest and wanted to explore without a care,
simply because it was there.
I started my walk on the sunniest of days,
the sun shone down with dappled rays.

As I walked through the evergreen wood,
the walk took longer than I knew it should.
The sun had gone, the moon appeared.
This is just what I had feared!

Colours of grey, black and the darkest green
I have ever seen.
The wind went through trees like a quiet waterfall.
The trees moved in around me, I heard their call.

I think I heard a ghostly cry
Out of the shadowy figures so high.
Might he get me? I shall see,
but as I turn around, it is just a tree!

What was that? I think it lightened.
Now I am really frightened.
Was that loud thunder?
Will I ever get out, I wonder?

I think my heart is beating like a train,
I can feel my blood begin to drain.
At last I hear a friendly laugh,
see my parents on the path.

'We were worried, where have you been?
Even though you are seventeen!
You must have been terrified, poor old lad.'
'I was not scared for a minute, Dad!'

Ben Hatfield (9)
St Anne's Catholic Primary School, Weeping Cross

I Have A Little Brother

I have a little brother, Peter is his name,
I have a little brother who drives us all insane.

I have a little brother whose hair is blond and brown,
I have a little brother who hates to go to town.

I have a little brother who lives at home with me,
I have a little brother who is nearly three.

I have a little brother who isn't really bad,
I have a little brother who is just plain mad.

I have a little brother who always screams and shouts,
I have a little brother who always runs about.

I have a little brother who likes the colour red,
I have a little brother who never goes to bed.

I have a little brother who is ever so funny,
I have a little brother who sleeps with a toy bunny.

I have a little brother who is always so jolly,
I have a little brother who rides in the shopping trolley.

I have a little brother who does a silly laugh,
I have a little brother who doesn't take a bath.

I have a little brother who is one big pest,
I have a little brother who really is the best.

I have a little brother who isn't very tame,
I have a little brother, I love him all the same.

Stephanie Barker (10)
St Anne's Catholic Primary School, Weeping Cross

Pets At Home

Our house is full of pets,
How many can you get?
Maka, Bobby and Jess too,
Toffee, Stray,
To name just a few.

Morpheus and the fish,
(24 of them),
All deep-fried,
Cor, what a dish!

Two dogs and a cat,
Strangely enough, not one rat.
Hamster and guinea pig,
Fish and snake,
How many do you think that makes?

Laura Osborne (10)
St Anne's Catholic Primary School, Weeping Cross

My Family

My mum shines like a star,
My dad drives a silver car,
My dog's called Holly
And my sister's jolly.
My fish are called Paul and John,
And they live in the pond.
We live together happily
As one big family!

Jade Connaughton (10)
St Anne's Catholic Primary School, Weeping Cross

On The Chase

Nature is a wonderful thing,
If you listen carefully, you can hear all the colourful birds sing.
On Cannock Chase there are animals and flowers too,
They all bring happiness to me and you.

In the winter the wind roars
And on the wind the birds soar.
The deer prance,
And if you look carefully, it looks like a flowing dance.

If you trip up on a rabbit's hole
You will fall on the ground and start to roll.
If there's a breeze, the bracken will start to sway
And the leaves all go away.

Pure purple heather against fern so green,
There is so much to be seen.
If you look up at the clouds so white,
A bird might disturb you during its flight.

Emma-May Harrison (10)
St Anne's Catholic Primary School, Weeping Cross

Children

One sunny day some children went out to play,
Girls and boys playing with all sorts of toys.

All day long, they have so much fun,
They always get hot running around in the sun.

They all go home to have something to eat.
They have so many games,
Such as guessing buildings' names.

Now it's the end of the day,
It's time to pack away!

Jodie Harris (9)
St Anne's Catholic Primary School, Weeping Cross

Homework Spell!

All: 'Homework, homework, such a bore
as if it's a permanent chore.'
1st witch: 'Homework never lets me see the light of day
when I want to go and play.'
2nd witch: 'Pens, pencils, rulers too,
swish them all down the loo.'
3rd witch: 'Teachers are always so mean,
especially Mr Dean.'
All: 'Homework, homework, such a bore
as if it's a permanent chore.'
All: 'Now this spell has all been done,
we all wish homework had never begun!'

Lauren Whitehouse (11)
St Luke's CE Primary School, Cannock

Uniform

Uniform, uniform, vile and smelly,
I would rather dress up in raspberry jelly.

All the teachers point and laugh,
then we realised they were completely naff.

The colours are manky and dull,
and our friend Frankie was driven to Hull.

Please, please, let us be trendy and cool,
and not look like scarecrow *fools*.

Uniform, uniform, vile and smelly,
I would rather dress up in a raspberry jelly.

James Tear (11)
St Luke's CE Primary School, Cannock

Uniform Spell

'Go away, away!' Yes, that's what I said,
you're all horrid and eerie and red.

I have to wear you Monday to Friday,
I'm glad it's the end of the week, I've survived the dismay!
On a weekend I wake up and shout, 'Hooray!'
It's the end of the week's dismay!

'Go away, away!' Yes, that's what I said,
you're all horrid and eerie and red.

Another Monday, oh, the pain!
If I had a chance, I'd plop you on the windowpane!
This is the end of my little rhyme,
oh my God, it's twenty-past nine.

'Go away, away!' Yes, that's what I said,
you're all horrid and eerie and red.

Oliver Rose (10)
St Luke's CE Primary School, Cannock

Spell To Get Rid Of School

Double, double, school's in trouble
Nothing left but stones and rubble.

Given homework every day
Haven't time to talk or play.

Punishments are so unfair
We've got no time to stand and stare.

Builder's plans were wrongly read
Knocked the building down instead.

Double, double, school's in trouble
Nothing left but stones and rubble.

Chris Allen (11)
St Luke's CE Primary School, Cannock

School

School, school, why are you here?
Six weeks holiday, that's not near.

School, we work, we talk, we study,
we have to be smart, not muddy.

We cannot chatter,
upstairs we can hear a patter.

Pens, pencils, sharpeners, rubbers and rulers,
in my school we cannot have foolers.

School, school, why are you here?
Six weeks holiday, that's not near.

Abby Sayers (10)
St Luke's CE Primary School, Cannock

School Spell

School, school, you are so cruel,
You always bring us to our doom.
Teachers' brains,
Badgers' spleens,
Fox with mange,
It's so strange.
Eye of newt,
Otter's foot,
Boy with hoop,
Olympic loop.
School, school, you are so cruel,
You always bring us to our doom.

Daniel Rose (10)
St Luke's CE Primary School, Cannock

Spell To Get Rid Of Little Brothers

Little brothers, always bad,
They run around and make you mad.
They nag, nag, nag, so here I brew
A potion to get rid of you!

Mix it up, stir it well,
Then watch your brother scream and yell.

Into the pot will go these things,
A mixture of small insect wings,
A rat's tail,
A fish scale,
A monkey eyeball too.
A hedgehog,
A large frog,
A lump of snotty goo.

Mix it up, stir it well,
Then watch your brother scream and yell.

When you've put in all that stuff,
Add a bit of hairy fluff,
And when you've thrown in lots of blood,
Then proceed to loads of mud.
Bake it hard,
Boil it hot,
Then stir it round your large black pot.

Mix it up, stir it well,
Then watch your brother scream and yell.

Add some venom,
Poison too,
A bar of soap
And gunky glue.
So little brother,
Please beware,
You're going to get
A shocking scare.

Joanna Bruce (10)
St Luke's CE Primary School, Cannock

The Magic Box

(Based on 'Magic Box' by Kit Wright)

In my magic box I am going to treasure . . .
The smell of wonderful and wondrous rainforests on a calm,
steady day,
The taste of a fresh, juicy, ripe pear from a new pear tree gleaming
in the sun,
The clattering of pretty, beautiful shells on the deep, golden shore.

In my magic box I am going to treasure . . .
The gentle, cold, steady breeze blowing on my cold face on a
breezy day,
The smell of new fresh leather on a chilly winter's night,
Baking scrumptious cream cakes in a scorching hot oven,
The smell spreading around a room.

In my magic box I am going to treasure . . .
The screeching of a violin in a special choir concert,
Fire smoke blowing strongly and fiercely in my face on a warm,
November night,
The tremendous loud noises of fireworks leaping up to the gleaming
dark sky.

In my magic box I am going to treasure . . .
The smell of the glorious season spring coming on a lovely sunny day,
The sizzling sound of sausages frying in a hot frying pan, travelling
Out of our window and into our garden.

In my magic box it is full of gleaming crystals, diamonds and jewels
That sparkle every minute.
I'll have many adventures, but the main adventure is
I will travel on a crystal dolphin's back through the horizon
And I will land calmly on my jewelled, spiral bed.

Emily Harris (10)
St Luke's CE Primary School, Cannock

School Uniform Spell!

See you soon, you old rags,
You make us look like carrier bags.

Some are long, some are short,
Please don't give us any more.

We don't like them, they make us sick,
Let's beat them up with a good old stick.

Rubbish red and boring blue,
Let's flush them all down the loo.

See you soon, you old rags,
You make us look like carrier bags.

Emily Fowler (11)
St Luke's CE Primary School, Cannock

Uniform

Begone, begone, you ugly rags,
You make us look like old rusty hags.

Slimy jumpers, cardigans too,
You made me flush you down the loo.

Sweaty shirts have been put on a curse
To make them smell even worse.

Then in summer, freaky frocks
Made from Granny's old table cloths.

Begone, begone, you ugly rags,
You make us look like old rusty hags.

Poppy Myatt (11)
St Luke's CE Primary School, Cannock

Spots Spell

Spots are yellow, spots are red,
They are things we always dread.

First take a puppy's bark,
Then the wings off a lark.
Next we take a horse's snort,
(Making sure we don't get caught).
Cat's miaow, hamster's squeak,
Then let it simmer for a week.
Boiling hot, freezing cold,
In a pot of brightest gold.

Spots are yellow, spots are red,
They are things we always dread.

Alysha Parry (11)
St Luke's CE Primary School, Cannock

Spell To Get Rid Of School

Bubble, bubble, you make me see double,
Why is school so much trouble?
Horrible homework, makes me boil,
Especially maths, it's a real toil.
Early mornings, short breaks,
It really give me the shakes.
So take my advice, don't go there,
It will really give you a scare.
Bubble, bubble, you make me see double,
Why is school so much trouble?

Megan Cranidge (10)
St Luke's CE Primary School, Cannock

Anti-School Spell

School, school, you cause me trouble,
You make my brain burn and bubble.

Burn down school by dragon's breath,
Destroying every last teacher's pet,
And ruin the play of Macbeth.

School, school, you cause me trouble,
You make my brain burn and bubble.

Sea horse spleen and black shark's fang,
Slime from the tentacles of Kodos and Kang,
And the power of Yin and Yang.

School, school, you cause me trouble,
You make my brain burn and bubble.

Sheepdog's liver and young lamb's heart,
Blood hawk's kidney and claw,
Burn the school into a giant jam tart.

School, school, you cause me trouble,
You make my brain burn and bubble.

Dragon's scale and monkey's paw,
The poison of snakes,
And finished off with a devil's claw.

School, school, you cause me trouble,
You make my brain burn and bubble.

Thomas Fowler (11)
St Luke's CE Primary School, Cannock

A Hypnosis Spell

Whatever I say will be done,
Whatever I say is number one.

Into the cauldron put a chocolate bar,
Also put a barrel of tar.
In the cauldron will also go
A desirable drop of winter snow.

Whatever I say will be done,
Whatever I say is number one.

In the cauldron goes now
A fresh drop of cold milk from a cow.
Also put the sharpest arrow,
Likewise to work it, a large size bow.

Whatever I say will be done,
Whatever I say is number one.

In the cauldron put a donkey tail,
A massive tongue of whale,
A full set of spider's legs will also go,
This chant will make thinking standards low.

Whatever I say will be done,
Whatever I say is number one.

Sam Shirley (10)
St Luke's CE Primary School, Cannock

The Magic Box

(Based on 'Magic Box' by Kit Wright)

I will capture in my box . . .
The last petal of a beautiful red rose,
A sparkling star which has fallen from the sky,
The first tweet of a newborn bird.

I will capture in my box . . .
The first squirrel to roam free,
The last smile to be made,
The first dream of a baby girl.

My box is created from velvet and silk,
With silver diamonds shaped like hearts,
Real gold hinges which look like stars.

I shall dance in my box
Or watch a sunset go down
Looking at the dolphins jumping out of the calm sea.

Abigail Whittingham (11)
St Luke's CE Primary School, Cannock

Mac-Brother

All: 'Double, double, brothers are trouble,
Their toes burn and then they bubble!'

Witch: 'Into the cauldron goes
The nail of a fox and golden locks,
Some spider's web,
Some horrid boy's leg,
Witch's mummy, maw and gulf,
Tongue of a dragon,
Tooth of a wolf.'

All: 'Double, double, brothers are trouble,
Their toes burn and then they bubble!'

Vicki Stevenson (10)
St Luke's CE Primary School, Cannock

The Magic Box

(Based on 'Magic Box' by Kit Wright)

I will capture in my box . . .
The last star to fall from space,
The first bird to sing and fly,
The last cloud to fall from the sky.

I will capture in my box . . .
The last feather off the robin,
The first egg to hatch off the chicken
The first girl to run freely.

My box is decorated in gold and silver,
With precious petals of red and white roses,
With dolphins and crystal snowflakes.

I shall glide in my box . . .
The first wish wished upon a star
And the first dream upon a child sleeping sweetly
And a world never seen before.

Samantha Barber (11)
St Luke's CE Primary School, Cannock

Garages

Garages are such noisy places,
Know what I mean?
Everyone seems to be
Playing darts, playing pool and messing around on table-top football.
I mean, it's like being in World War III.

Garages are such crowded places,
Know what I mean?
Everyone seems to be
Dumping stuff, chucking stuff on the floor and messing around.
I mean, it's like being on a crowded bus,
Know what I mean?

James Hughes (11)
St Luke's CE Primary School, Cannock

The Magic Box

(Based on 'Magic Box' by Kit Wright)

I will store in my magic box . . .
The wavy blue sea swishing around,
The warm, smooth sand upon the beach,
The palm trees moving wildly with the wind.

I will store in my magic box . . .
Fresh, tasty ice cream just coming from the cold freezer,
Sizzling brown burgers coming from the BBQ,
Lovely smelling flowers growing from the ground.

I will store in my magic box . . .
A cool lemonade with ice coming from the fridge,
A warm, fluffy teddy from the end of my bed,
A picture of a cosy family sitting on comfy sofa.

I will store in my magic box . . .
A postman posting mail with a dog barking back,
A loud rip of Sellotape unwrapping in a room,
Lids popping off pens once you start to write.

I will store in my magic box . . .
A noisy, loud radio coming through big speakers,
Big cars going past making the ground vibrate,
Lamp post on the street switching as they go off,
That's what I would put in my magic box!

Faith McKenzie (10)
St Luke's CE Primary School, Cannock

The Magic Box

(Based on 'Magic Box' by Kit Wright)

I will put in my box . . .
The sound of birdsong on an early morning dawn,
The sizzling sound of bacon drifting upstairs,
The shock of a cold wind smacking my frozen. face.

I will put in my box . . .
The strong smell of flowers in my rough hands,
The feeling of thick, soft, fluffy wool wrapped around me,
The taste of freezing cold water pouring down my dry throat.

I will put in my box . . .
Children's laughter screeching in the playground,
The taste of hot, sickly school dinners splattered on my plate,
My aching hand after a hard, painful day's work.

I will put in my box . . .
The shimmering of the silver ocean,
A dolphin leaping out of the gleaming sea,
The closing of my eye after an exhausting day.

My box is decorated with glitter as the gleaming ocean,
The blooming of flowers and all my friends' names written in Chinese.
That is my magic box.

Alexandra Dowell (10)
St Luke's CE Primary School, Cannock

My Magic Box

(Based on 'Magic Box' by Kit Wright)

I will put in my box . . .
The reflection of a delicate diamond sparkling stunningly in the summer sunlight,
The smell of chocolate cake freshly out of the red-hot burning oven.

I will put in my box . . .
The touch of a fluffy blanket when it softly brushes your bare legs,
The feeling of the gooey cake mixture before it is baked.

I will put in my box . . .
The dust of an angel tickling your head,
The enjoyment when I hear my favourite song bursting through the speakers.

I will put in my box . . .
A silver unicorn that shines like a star,
The taste of toffee touching my tongue,
The thought of a plant sprouting a flower.

I will put in my box . . .
The bright twinkle of a star in the dark night,
The colours of the rainbow twinkling in the sunlight,
The feather of a golden eagle,
The scale of a mermaid.

My box is silver with crystal tears on top and fairy dust at the sides,
Pixies hiding in the corners,
I would like to crawl softly along a spider's web along its silky rim
And end up in an enchanted forest
Riding a pearly-white horse with silky white hair.

Poppy Flynn (10)
St Luke's CE Primary School, Cannock

The Magic Box

(Based on 'Magic Box' by Kit Wright)

I will put in my magic box . . .
The sight of a newly born chick
The taste of a chocolate chip cookie
The smell of Dad's freshly baked bread.

I will put in my magic box . . .
The twinkle of a golden star
The scent of a newborn plant
The sparkling teeth of David Beckham.

I will put in my magic box . . .
The sizzle of a burger on the BBQ
The shine of the golden rail in my aunt's house
The trickle of blood when you have been pricked by a rose.

I will put in my magic box . . .
The whiff of a baker's shop in the winter
The tingle of a new silver bed
The bite of a little baby.

I will put in my magic box . . .
The first block of a new Cadbury's chocolate bar
The stink of my old gym socks
The word that you screamed.

I will fashion my box . . .
In every corner I will put my friends
In the centre I will put a blade of grass from Old Trafford
On the top I will put a feather of a golden eagle.

Ryan Goodwin (10)
St Luke's CE Primary School, Cannock

The Magic Box

(Based on 'Magic Box' by Kit Wright)

I will put in my magic box . . .
The feel of the skin from a slimy snake's back,
The smell of my mum's steamy roast dinner drifting through the kitchen door,
The smoke of the bonfire on Bonfire Night.

I will put in my magic box . . .
The sound of the first baby bird singing at dawn,
The kettle bubbling over the boil
The taste of newly made apple pie with custard.

I will put in my magic box . . .
The strong and fierce smell of hairspray,
The freshly picked blackberries from a prickly tree,
The first flight of a newborn butterfly.

I will put in my box . . .
The smell of fresh winter air,
The feel of soft clouds in the sky,
The feel of cold snow.

I will put in my box . . .
The pitter-patter of raindrops
The smell of freshly baked hot buns
The feel of fresh soil.

Amanda Cole-Ward (11)
St Luke's CE Primary School, Cannock

My Magic Box

(Based on 'Magic Box' by Kit Wright)

I will put in my magic box . . .
The sound of dolphins jumping into the sea,
The sunset over the horizon,
The touch of a silky curtain.

I will put in my magic box . . .
The smell of a roasting turkey,
The taste of a juicy marshmallow,
The sound of singing birds.

I will put in my magic box . . .
The sight of Wayne Rooney's goals
The atmosphere of a screaming crowd,
The smell of a fresh, grassy air.

I will put in my magic box . . .
The feel of a crusty autumn leaf,
The smell of conkers,
And the sight of spiky shells.

The corners of my magic box are made from cooled lava,
The top is a thick layer of snow,
In the middle is a diamond wave,
My friends' and heroes' names cover the sides.

Ashley Wilson (10)
St Luke's CE Primary School, Cannock

The Magic Box

(Based on 'Magic Box' by Kit Wright)

I will put in my box . . .
The smell of freshly baked chocolate sponge cake coming out of the oven,
The sight of my breath on a freezing cold morning,
The feeling of my warm cat's fur rubbing the side of my feet.

I will put in my box . . .
The sound of an ice-cold snowman with a rumbling belly,
The delivery and enjoyment of my favourite song bursting through the speakers,
The touch of an angel stroking the side of my face on a dark, gloomy night.

I will put in my box . . .
The reflection of a delicate diamond sparkling stunningly in the summer sun,
The dust of the first fairy in the land,
The violent wishes spoken in Gujarati.

My box is created with diamonds with gold and silver gems inside
With pixie dust sprinkled on the top,
Fairies hiding away in the corners,
I would ride my palomino in my box
And land gracefully on the Caribbean beach.

Jessica Evans (11)
St Luke's CE Primary School, Cannock

My Magic Box

(Based on 'Magic Box' by Kit Wright)

I will put in my box . . .
The smell of the creamy, melting chocolate cooking in the kitchen,
My first ever crackle of a sound as a baby,
The feel of a warm and gentle first kiss.

I will put in my box . . .
The pittering and pattering of the delicate, white snow on my face,
The wobbling effect of a newly set jelly,
A fish swimming and diving in the calm, settled sea.

I will put in my box . . .
The soft velvet touch of a horse's nostrils,
The brightly shining, glistening sun,
The first sound of a galloping Red Rum pony.

My box has lilac silk for the lid,
The hinges are like a chest of gold,
I've got fairy dust sprinkled all around.

In my box I'll gallop on my newborn pony
And I'll sit in the glistening sunshine eating my creamy,
melting chocolate.

Jade Golby (10)
St Luke's CE Primary School, Cannock

My Magic Box

(Based on 'Magic Box' by Kit Wright)

I will put in my magic box . . .
The crackle of a fire on a cold winter's night,
The scent of bacon for my breakfast,
The sight of a shiny red ruby.

I will put in my magic box . . .
The taste of butter on popcorn,
The whirling eye of a tornado,
The heat of the burning sun.

I will put in my magic box . . .
The idea of a modern car,
The view of a some cute little kittens,
The taste of a well done roast chicken.

I will put in my magic box . . .
The scent of fresh lavender,
The knowledge of all,
The enjoyment of playing video games.

I will pull out of my magic box . . .
The dark and evil side,
The bad pollution in the ocean,
The bad pollution in the air.

Charlie Summers (10)
St Luke's CE Primary School, Cannock

My Magic Box

(Based on 'Magic Box' by Kit Wright)

I will put in my magic box . . .
The smell of freshly baked cakes
The scene of the sun setting down on a cold night,
The sound of the waves in the sea.

I will treasure in my magic box . . .
The stunning view across the fields on a frosty morning,
The sound of rain hitting my window
The smell in the Chase after it's rained.

I will store in my magic box . . .
The feel of the moon looking down on me,
The taste of a crunchy apple pie,
The sound of the wind blowing through the trees.

I will place in my magic box . . .
The sound of sizzling bacon,
The feel of shiny silk,
The sound of the first giggle of a baby.

I will keep in my magic box . . .
The feel of snow falling on my head
The smell of onions spitting in a pan
The taste of melted chocolate.

Chloë Gillett (11)
St Luke's CE Primary School, Cannock

My Magic Box

(Based on 'Magic Box' by Kit Wright)

I will put in my box . . .
The stink of Mr Thornhill's football socks,
The feel of a bushy tail of a fox,
The itchiness of chickenpox.

I will put in my box . . .
The taste of burgers straight off a flaring barbecue,
The explosion of bubblegum,
The sound of chanting at a football match.

I will put in my box . . .
The smell of a freshly baked cake cooking in the oven,
The enjoyment of playing with Roberto Carlos,
The sadness of dying.

I will put in my box . . .
The brightest flash of lightning,
The first ever eclipse,
One scale of a fish.

The fashion of my box . . .
Every corner of my box will have cobwebs,
The hinges on my box will be my very first teeth,
My box will be made of gleaming silver and gold.

David Rochelle (10)
St Luke's CE Primary School, Cannock

The Magic Box

(Based on 'Magic Box' by Kit Wright)

I will put in my magic box. . .
The sound of my first word I ever whispered,
The sight of a white snowman walking,
Also a golden sun when it is setting and shining in the sky.

I will put in my magic box . . .
The goodness of the world,
A flower shooting out of its root,
The blossom of a tree sprinkling down.

I will put in my magic box . . .
The cry of a newborn baby,
The kindness of a puppy-dog playing with his owner sweetly,
The smell of a freshly baked cake.

I will put in my magic box . . .
A man walking along a bright, colourful rainbow glistening in the sky,
A smiling moon in the night sky's glow,
A shimmering, sparkling fairy making somebody's wish come true.

I will put in my magic box . . .
A chirping chick hatching from its nest,
A bright, shining light upon the Earth,
The soft feel of a little kitten.

Nicole Tapper (11)
St Luke's CE Primary School, Cannock

My Magic Box

(Based on 'Magic Box' by Kit Wright)

I will treasure in my magic box . . .
The feel of a hot, fiery dragon's breath,
The taste of hot melted chocolate,
The sizzle of a sausage in the oven.

I will keep in my magic box . . .
The little roar of a baby lion getting louder and louder,
The sparkle of the stars shooting and sparkling all night,
A snowman melting in the winter sun.

I will put in my magic box . . .
The crispiness of my Rice Krispies in the morning,
A dolphin jumping out of the crystal-blue sea,
The squeak of a pen on a whiteboard.

My box is fashioned with ice and snow,
With a red crystal diamond of my grandmother's necklace
And the sprinkle of fairy dust all over.

I shall jump in my box and sail on the open sea,
Go ice skating in my box so no one sees me,
I will hide in my box downstairs in my living room
So I can listen to my mum and dad's secrets.

Chloe Goy (11)
St Luke's CE Primary School, Cannock

The Magic Box

(Based on 'Magic Box' by Kit Wright)

I will put in my box . . .
The howl of a wolf on a moonlit night,
The feel of the sand between my toes,
The honk of a steamboat setting off across the horizon.

I will put in my box . . .
The school bell telling kids it's home time,
The squeal of a baby wanting its dinner,
The metal clanging noise of spoons knocking together.

I will put in my box . . .
The taste of a freshly picked Braeburn,
The scream of a friendly ghost wanting a friend,
The blinding sight of a rising sun.

My box is fashioned from dragon's skin to seal blubber,
With a big, red sun on the lid
And the hinges made from solid gold.

In my box I'll fly to the moon and find things that nobody's found,
Then I'll come back crashing into the sea,
Luckily it's a boat as well.

Adam Williams (11)
St Luke's CE Primary School, Cannock

My Magic Box

(Based on 'Magic Box' by Kit Wright)

I will treasure in my box . . .
The refreshing smell of my mum's perfume,
In my box I will put the hugs of my mum and dad
I will hold in my box the yummy taste of Chinese and Indian food.

I will keep in my box . . .
The feel of my dog's silky fur when he has been combed,
The sound of footsteps walking on the surface of pure white snow,
The cheer of the crowd when Wolves score,
The tickling of the sand when you walk on it.

I will hold still in my box . . .
The fresh smell of Haze citrus air-freshener,
The smell of freshly baked garlic bread,
The feel of a soft, delicate rose petal.

My box is gold and pink with the reflection of blue diamonds
And bright silver swirls shining like stars on a dark, dark night.

Hayley Butler (10)
St Luke's CE Primary School, Cannock

My Magic Box

(Based on 'Magic Box' by Kit Wright)

I will put in my magic box . . .
The tingling of my brightly polished bicycle bell,
The galloping of horses echoing through a long, dark tunnel,
The swishing of a velvet dress on a winter's night.

I will put in my magic box . . .
The swish of the trees blowing in the autumn wind,
The reflection of a sparkling diamond in the summer sun,
The freshly baked cakes being iced in the kitchen.

My magic box is decorated with pink feathers,
Sparkling diamonds and light pink velvet,
The hinges are silver, glittering spider webs with swirls in the corners.

In my magic box I will wear sparkling diamonds in my hair,
I'll wear a velvet dress on a galloping horse,
Around me there are trees swishing in the breeze,
The smell of freshly baked cakes and icing over a grassy hill.

Natasha Plant (10)
St Luke's CE Primary School, Cannock

My Magic Box

(Based on 'Magic Box' by Kit Wright)

I will put in my magic box . . .
The feeling of an elastic band snapping in my hands,
The first word I ever whispered,
The sight of an eclipse in the middle of the day,
The quacking sound of a duck.

I will put in my magic box . . .
The light of the sun at sunset,
The peace at school when everybody is working quietly,
The look of freshly baked bread as I'm carrying it in from the kitchen,
The shock of an electric shock.

I will put in my magic box . . .
The smell of the rain after it hails on a Sunday morning,
The words of a Frenchman when asked for directions,
The screaming of my mum having a baby,
The loudness of a plane taking off.

I will put in my magic box . . .
The coldness of the white snow on Christmas Day,
The soft, cuddly fur of my cats while I'm stroking their heads,
The barking of my little puppy-dog,
The number of spots on a cow.

I will put in my magic box . . .
The taste of the cold ice cream on my burning tongue,
The swish of a silk sari on a summer night
The shrill of a harshly blown postman's whistle,
The crackling of a firework on Bonfire Night.

Samantha Rocks (10)
St Luke's CE Primary School, Cannock

The Magic Box

(Based on 'Magic Box' by Kit Wright)

I will put in my box . . .
The smell of freshly baked bread sneaking through the crack of the
steamed-up window,
The sound of a newborn kitten squealing for food,
The shimmer in the water as a frog jumps in the rippling reflection
of itself.

I will put in my box . . .
The sound of the sea splashing up the sharp, ridgy rocks,
The feeling of soft, smooth hand cream sliding across your hands,
The sound of a horse going clippety-clop, galloping down the road.

I will put in my box . . .
The swaying of water trickling past your feet,
The sound of music banging and vibrating out of the speakers,
The sound of leaves in autumn crackling beneath your feet.

I will put in my box . . .
The twinkling of fairy lights upon the Christmas tree,
The crunching of snow as I make a snowman,
The sweet smell of Comfort in my newly made bed.

I will put in my box . . .
The smell of Mum's perfume as she cuddles me goodnight,
The sound of bells bouncing from side to side in St Luke's church,
The feeling of the softness and fluffiness of my fleecy blanket.

Laura Braden (10)
St Luke's CE Primary School, Cannock

The Magic Box

(Based on 'Magic Box' by Kit Wright)

I will put in my magic box . . .
The mixture of my favourite chocolate bar,
The smell of freshly baked bread,
The treasure out of a treasure chest box.

I will put in my magic box . . .
The golden sun disappearing over the horizon,
The echo of singing down the alleyway,
The pattern of my breath on a cold, cold morning.

I will put in my magic box . . .
The gentle fur of my new puppy-dog,
The touch of newly picked apples off the tree,
The crunchy taste of a pear.

I will put in my magic box . . .
All of the birds I've got,
My favourite car, which is a Vauxhall Astra
And a pond with fish swimming in it.

I will put I my magic box . . .
The Eiffel Tower in France,
The taste of apple pie freshly baked,
The Manchester United football ground.

Leigh-Amanda Jones (10)
St Luke's CE Primary School, Cannock

The Magic Box

(Based on 'Magic Box' by Kit Wright)

I will put in my box . . .
The crying of a newborn baby,
The noise of a tree swirling in the air.

I will place in my box . . .
The roar of a dinosaur,
The croak of a dying dog,
The swish of a bird's wing.

I will store in my box . . .
The crash of a wave coming down on the rocks,
The scream of a whale in pain,
The song coming from a choir.

My box is patterned with glitter and shine,
The brightness of a gem,
The colour of the sun.

I will dive in my box . . .
All the seas in the world,
All the animals I want
And my friends.

Christopher Lee (10)
St Luke's CE Primary School, Cannock

Danielle's Magic Box

(Based on 'Magic Box' by Kit Wright)

I will capture in my box . . .
The first light of the last firework,
A scale from a rainbowfish,
The dream of a runaway princess.

I will capture in my box . . .
The laughter of a child running free,
The first fallen autumn leaf,
A drop of water from the seven seas.

My box is decorated with diamonds, rubies, emeralds and sapphires,
It's made of gold, silver and ice,
The lock is made of crystal glass and the corners made of dew.

I shall snowboard in my box
On the great, high Mount Everest
And then fall and land on snow like a newborn lamb's wool.

Danielle Mayo (11)
St Luke's CE Primary School, Cannock

The Magic Box

(Based on 'Magic Box' by Kit Wright)

I will capture in my box . . .
A thick tropical bright rainbow
The heat of a cosy fire,
The tip of a tongue reaching a creamy ice cream.

I will capture in my box . . .
A giant African elephant in the sun,
One of the softest clouds floating in the sky,
The first puppy born on Earth.

My box is designed by a collage of colours
With velvet red material and golden stars.

I will play in my box with my friends and family
And I will roam freely.
I will love my box!

Molly Gough (11)
St Luke's CE Primary School, Cannock

My Magic Box

(Based on 'Magic Box' by Kit Wright)

I will place in my box . . .
The greatest goal scored in history
A priest on a camel
The worst killing spider in the world.

I will place in my box . . .
Hinges of a magic door,
The first star I saw in the sky,
A magic key which opens a new world.

My box is decorated with diamonds twinkling on the side
Emeralds sparkling on the lid
Rubies dreaming in the corners.

I will fly in my box . . .
To a faraway land with an exotic jungle
To a place that's not been found.

Cameron Fergusson (11)
St Luke's CE Primary School, Cannock

The Magic Box

(Based on 'Magic Box' by Kit Wright)

I will capture in my box . . .
The last mammoth ever to roam the Earth,
The thoughts of a British soldier in the war before he dies,
A smouldering piece of rock from the first fire.

I will capture in my box . . .
The first red leaf ever to fall off a tree in autumn,
A horn from the oldest triceratops,
A segment from a ruby dug up years ago.

My box is fashioned from fire and gold,
With sapphire keys to lock it.

I will travel in my box to foreign lands
And then dive deep down into the sea.

Jonathan Kirk (10)
St Luke's CE Primary School, Cannock

Kirstie's Magic Box

(Based on 'Magic Box' by Kit Wright)

I will capture for my box . . .
The tears from a wartime evacuee,
The first leap of a spring lamb,
The last sigh of a dying cat.

I will capture for my box . . .
A spaceship full of aliens from infinity and beyond,
The anger from a charging bull,
The first man on the moon,
The last bone from a dinosaur.

I will capture for my box . . .
The first tropical bud to open,
The music from a church choir,
The first note from a new recorder.

My box is created by the glitter from the stars,
And the magic from Harry Potter's wand
And the secrets from far distant lands
I shall swim in my box to when dinosaurs were alive
And when you could roam freely without being mugged
I shall swim to lands not yet discovered.

Kirstie Swann (11)
St Luke's CE Primary School, Cannock

My Magic Box

(Based on 'Magic Box' my Kit Wright)

I will capture in my box . . .
The first time a baby cries,
The last smile of an old caring friend,
The smell of a new book.

I will place in my box . . .
A star that's faded and lonely,
A taste of hot apple pie,
A single bud from a wild rose.

I will lock in my box . . .
The escaping smell of fresh baking bread,
The song of a newborn bird,
And an everlasting polite welcome.

My box is designed with dolphins and starfish,
Its hinges are made from tiger's teeth,
Its edges are sealed with tight kisses and secrets.

I will dive in my box where the sun shines red in the biggest pool ever,
Then float in a bubble the colour of the sea.

Jade Griffiths (10)
St Luke's CE Primary School, Cannock

The Magic Box

(Based on 'Magic Box' by Kit Wright)

I will put in my box . . .
The sound of kids at the park,
The sight of snowy mountains,
The smell of a summer's day.

I will put in my box . . .
The lovely fur of a dog,
The excitement of winning,
The cloud of my breath on a cold winter's day.

I will put in my box . . .
The feeling of a hot bath
The sight of the deep blue sea,
Looking back at an achievement.

My box is fashioned with colourful patterns
My rims are the bones of a giant,
The inside has cushioned sides.

I will put in my box . . .
The feeling of meeting an alien
The sound of rain pattering on the window,
The twinkling lights below from the aeroplane window.

I will put in my box . . .
The thrill of Christmas morning
The heart-stopping moment leaping into a cold pool
The taste of a crunchy apple.

Edward Fleet (10)
St Luke's CE Primary School, Cannock

The Magic Box

(Based on 'Magic Box' by Kit Wright)

In my box I will put . . .
The smell of crispy bacon floating through the air,
The taste of freshly baked Bramley apple pie,
The shimmering reflection of a dazzling diamond.

In my box I will put . . .
The feeling of a chilling wind freezing my ears on a winter's day,
The gentle bubbling of an Aero melting in my mouth,
The sight of an eclipse dazzling in my eyes every millennium.

In my box I will put . . .
The twinkle of a star on a dark, dark night,
The last roar of a dying dinosaur,
The ivory tusk of the last ever elephant.

In my box I will put . . .
The crackle of a fire on a cold winter's night,
The taste of a freezing cold ice cream on a summer's day,
The eyes of a one-day-old puppy gleaming in the sun.

In my box I will put . . .
The taste of a first fatty burger from McDonald's,
The scent of a first rose that ever came to Earth,
The taste of a newly picked crunchy apple.

Luke Rushbrook (10)
St Luke's CE Primary School, Cannock

The Magic Box

(Based on 'Magic Box' by Kit Wright)

I will capture in my box . . .
The last shining star in the night sky,
The first snowflake to fall in winter,
A teardrop from the hurling phoenix.

I will capture in my box . . .
A magic unicorn from my dreams,
The first angel in the sky,
A wish from Aladdin's cave.

I will capture in my box . . .
The voice of a nightingale,
A magic carpet from my bedtime stories,
A golden apple for life's sweet dreams.

My box is made from fine oak trees
From pearls and rubies from the oceans and seas
Embroidered with patterns from golden leaves
This is my box for all to see.

I will travel the world and the seven seas
Discover lost cities, just my box and me.

Kelly-Ann Smith (11)
St Luke's CE Primary School, Cannock

My Magic Box

(Based on 'Magic Box' by Kit Wright)

I will put in my magic box . . .
The singing, shiny sun disappearing into the darkness,
A robin twittering in the cold winter evening,
The heat of a brightly burning fire in the mansion house.

I will put in my magic box . . .
The feel of sand running through my feet when I first went to the beach,
The taste of ice cream on a summer's day
The noise of a puppy's bark.

I will put in my magic box . . .
The shine of the moon in the dark night,
The smell of chocolate cake in the kitchen,
The sound of the sea crashing against the rocks.

My magic box is fashioned with the finest silk
With pixie dust on the lid, with twinkling stars in the corners,
I shall travel in my magic box to faraway places
Then ride on a dolphin's back and wash ashore
onto a sunny yellow beach.

Georgia Duggan (11)
St Luke's CE Primary School, Cannock

The Magic Box

(Based on 'Magic Box' by Kit Wright)

I will put in my magic box . . .
The smell of petrol flowing into a tank,
The feel of velvet fabric swishing on my body,
The crunchy popcorn in my mouth.

I will put in my magic box . . .
The freezing snow melting in my hand softly,
The end of a summer's day that's not too warm and not too cool,
The G forces on a ride.

I will put in my magic box . . .
My worst word I screeched out loud,
The warm water of a bath surrounding me,
My cloudy, frosty breath on a cold autumn morning.

My box is covered with gold and silver,
Sparkly glitter twinkling in the light secured with a padlock.
Gold corners of the box,
So bright and beautiful you can see yourself,
All bright and beautiful, all ready for me.

Alex Woolliscroft (11)
St Luke's CE Primary School, Cannock

Cats

Fur-licker
Mouse-chaser
Curtain-catcher
Window-sitter
Fire-napper
Whisker-flicker
Chicken-nicker
Toy-player.

Daniel Howell (10)
St Martin's CE Primary School, Bradley

Fear

Fear is darkness in the night
Fear is a bang on the door
Fear is frightening everywhere
Fear is a growl and a roar
Fear is a scary moment
Fear tastes sour
Fear is footsteps in the dark
Fear is talking to dead people
Fear is so scary you sweat
Fear is an attacking pet
Fear is when you wet your pants
Fear is a screaming girl
Fear is a place where you are lost
Fear is a place where you never come out alive
But most of all that fear will soon come to you
Because fear is everywhere.

Chelsea Sillitto (9)
St Martin's CE Primary School, Bradley

Budgie

Noise-maker
Mess-maker
Sand-scratcher
Bell-knocker
Water-splasher
Mirror-basher
Head-stander
Chirp-chirper.

Daniel Whitehouse & Lee Hale (10)
St Martin's CE Primary School, Bradley

Love

Love is when my baby brother smiles at me when I come home
from school.
Love is like some tall, pretty roses growing in the summer gardens.
Love is for some beautiful bluebells growing in the fields.
Love is when I see the warm swimming baths.
Love is when my mom brought me an expensive bracelet.
Love is when my mom smiles at me when I go into school.
Love is when my brother gave me his best trophy.
Love is when a red love heart fills the air with romance.
Love is summertime when flowers are growing and the sun is shining.
Love is when my little brother hugs me when I come out of school.

Jade Pattison (9)
St Martin's CE Primary School, Bradley

Sadness

Sadness is dark blackness when you're by yourself.
Sadness is when I have to go shopping.
Sadness is lava coming out of a volcano.
Sadness is dark blue when you're in a blue room with a stranger.
Sadness is when someone dies in your family.
Sadness is when people pick on me.
Sadness is when your best mates are not your friends anymore.

Amberjade Taylor (9)
St Martin's CE Primary School, Bradley

Happiness

Happiness is butterflies and red roses under the tree of green.
Happiness is gold treasure in a treasure chest.
Happiness is when my nan loves me and lets me have some sweets.
Happiness is when the sun's out and I can go on holiday
to the swimming pool.
Happiness is when it's a Christmas disco and we have 2 weeks
holiday.

Rebecca Hassell (9)
St Martin's CE Primary School, Bradley

Love

Love is for a red heart that fills the air with romance.
Love is for orange flowers growing in the fields.
Love is for a boy and girl holding hands.
Love is for two adults going on a date.
Love is for me giving my dad a hug.
Love is for the shape of a love heart.
Love is for someone getting married in a church.

Don't you think there is a lot of love?

Emily Paterson (8)
St Martin's CE Primary School, Bradley

Happiness

Happiness is the red roses growing in the garden.
Happiness is the yellow sun in the sky.
Happiness is when I see my nan and grandad.
Happiness is the smell of lamb cooking in the oven.
Happiness is when my cat cuddles up to me
when I come back home from school.
Happiness is when England score a goal
and I am full of *happiness*.

Corey Tudor (8)
St Martin's CE Primary School, Bradley

Hate

I hate my door because it squeaks.
I hate my room because it is small.
I hate my skateboard, it is too big.
I hate my TV because it is broken
And my blanket because it is itchy.
I hate my shoes because they are ripped.
I hate my bed because it is cold.
I am full of hate.

Hayden Smith (9)
St Martin's CE Primary School, Bradley

What Can You See In The Army?

What can you see?
The rocket launcher going *bang!*
What can you feel?
If you were there you'd be scared.
What can you hear?
You can hear machine guns
Firing to shoot the baddies, killing them all.

What can you see?
I can see a man shooting!
What can you feel?
I can feel the gun shaking.
What can you hear?
I can hear the machine guns firing.

Jack Mansell (7)
St Martin's CE Primary School, Bradley

Fear

Fear is the howling of a dog in the dark night.
Fear is footsteps on creaking wooden floorboards
and fire burning in the fields.
Fear is when your baby brother or sister
wakes you up screaming in the middle of the dark night.
Fear is when you wake up in the middle of the dark, lonely night
and no one else is awake.
Fear is when you're round someone's house
and someone has had an accident in your family.
Fear is when you have a bad nightmare and you wake up screaming.
Fear is when you hear banging on your bedroom door
in the dark, lonely night.
Fear is when you are lost in the middle of nowhere.

Isabelle Blewitt (8)
St Martin's CE Primary School, Bradley

Bad Pets

I had a cat,
That was very fat,
He never moved,
He was always soothed,
By lying on my dad's hat.

I had a dog,
That lived in a log,
She chased the cats,
Ran from rats
And fell in the city bog.

I had a mouse,
He had his own house,
He never stopped moving,
When he was grooving,
With the neighbour's woodlouse.

Ryan Tunstall (10)
St Martin's CE Primary School, Bradley

Fear

Fear is when you are walking down a pitch-black alley.
Fear is when you are in the middle of a field and it is as black
as the road.
Fear is when someone is about to grab you tight.
Fear is when someone has taken you away far.
Fear is when someone bangs on the door.
Fear is when you have a gun to your head.
Fear is when you are watching an over 18s film.
Fear is a whip going around your face.
Fear is when someone hits you hard.
Fear is when you are going to get shot.

Joe Davies (9)
St Martin's CE Primary School, Bradley

Dog

Clever-escaper
Hole-digger
Noise-maker
Window-jumper
Trouble-maker
Book-ripper
Mud-roller
Food-stealer
Bird-chaser
Sweet-stealer.

Chelsea Lees (10)
St Martin's CE Primary School, Bradley

Ice Cream

I like ice cream,
I think it seems the right ice cream,
Do you like it too?
All different flavours,
Which ones are your best flavours?
I like to lick it.
Sophie likes to kiss it.

Hayleigh Atkinson (8)
St Martin's CE Primary School, Bradley

Pets

P rancing to and fro on my wall,
E veryone said it'd never get tall,
T aking all the food to eat,
S itting on the floor smelling people's feet.

Paige Strong (11) & Tony McCarthy (10)
St Martin's CE Primary School, Bradley

Spring

Flower-opener,
Heat-giver,
Sun-shiner,
Bird-flutterer,
Tree-bloomer,
Egg-giver,
Jesus-crucifier,
Outdoor-player.

Kirsty Brown, Leanne Tanner & Leanne Timmins (11)
St Martin's CE Primary School, Bradley

Ice Creams

Ice creams are creamy
It's really dreamy,
It tastes so creamy
On a hot summer's day.
There is nothing better to eat.
Chocolate, minty,
Strawberry ice cream.
You can't resist it
I don't just like it,
I really like it,
More than
Anything.

Amy Henderson (8)
St Martin's CE Primary School, Bradley

Pets Are Great

P roud to be your friend
E ager to see you
T rying its best to beat the rest
S o full of joy.

David Briscoe (9)
St Martin's CE Primary School, Bradley

In The Playground

In the playground
Kick the ball,
Hit it off your head
In the playground.

The playground,
It is enormous,
So you can hide anywhere,
In the playground.

In the playground
Be polite,
Say wonderful things
In the playground.

Shannon Salter (10)
St Martin's CE Primary School, Bradley

Cats And Dogs Playing

Dogs and cats wearing black and white fur coats
Dogs and cats playing in front of the fire
Dogs and cats going anywhere their master goes.

Cats playing with string
Dogs playing with plastic bones
Dogs burying bones underground.

Dogs smell people on their patch
If anyone goes there
They will rip them to pieces!

Pieces, pieces, no one will go
Where that fierce cat and dog are!

Marc Powell (10)
St Martin's CE Primary School, Bradley

School Senses

I wake up in the morning before I get to school
I smell . . .
Toast burning,
Tea smelling,
Hairspray flaring,
Perfume scented,
Gel sticking.

I wake up in the morning when I get to school
I hear . . .
'Inney minney maca raca.'
'I did this, I did that.'
'I've got a cat, I've got a new hat.'
'Chatter, chatter.'
'Ha ha.'

I wake up in the morning when I get to school
I see . . .
Girls doing cartwheels,
Boys playing football,
Teachers chattering,
Girls and boys staring on,
Parents talking all day long.

Shannon Edwards (9)
St Martin's CE Primary School, Bradley

My Holiday

Sitting on the beach
Having some sweets
Swimming in the pool
Getting cool.

Eating a lolly
In the shape of a lorry
I had a sunbathe
My mate got hit by a wave.

Ben Pearce (9)
St Martin's CE Primary School, Bradley

There Is A Monster In My Locker

There is a monster in my locker
And I don't know what to do
There is a monster in my locker
And I need the loo
There is a scary monster in my locker
Help, help please.

There is a monster in my locker
Now I know what to do
There is a monster in my locker
Now I don't want the zoo
That monster has disappeared . . .
'Wahoo! Wahoo!'

Curtis Nicholls (9)
St Martin's CE Primary School, Bradley

I Love Pets

I love pets,
Pets love me,
Dogs and cats and fishes,
With a woof, woof here,
And a miaow, miaow there,
Now I have pets everywhere!

Lauren Archer (9)
St Martin's CE Primary School, Bradley

Hate

Hate is when I stomp up the stairs and slam the doors.
Hate is where I kick the walls.
Hate is where I throw my toys.
Hate is where there is a gang of boys.

Ryan James (8)
St Martin's CE Primary School, Bradley

Weird World Wonders

Imagine, imagine,
Dragons swimming underwater.
Imagine, imagine,
A flying kangaroo.
Imagine, imagine,
A talking fish.
Imagine, imagine,
A kangaroo beaver,
Oh what a weird place.

Imagine, imagine,
A duck underwater.
Imagine, imagine,
A flying dog.
Imagine, imagine,
A talking elephant.
Imagine, imagine,
A jumping crab.
Oh what a weird place.

Mitchel Jeavons (10)
St Martin's CE Primary School, Bradley

Family Chaos

Chitter-chatters
Clitter-clatters
Pitter-patters
Food-fighters
Big-biters
Nasty-namers
Sweet-stealers
Potato-peelers
And *crash!*

Mitchell Pearson & Ryan Westwood (11)
St Martin's CE Primary School, Bradley

My Rabbit

Hole-digger
Nose-twitcher
Nibble-maker
Pain-maker
Munching-eater.

Cleveland McGrory (10)
St Martin's CE Primary School, Bradley

My Bayley

My dog is cute, she is a golden cocker spaniel
She jumps up you for fuss
She snaps and growls when you try to take her bone off her
She is beautiful.

Dogs are beautiful
She gets red-hot because she has got a big coat
The dog's ears are long.

Mine all mine, dogs are
In the sun my dog plays with me
No, you can't have my dog
My dog's ears are as soft as silk.

Cameron Blewitt (9)
St Martin's CE Primary School, Bradley

The Wind

The wind, the wind
What is it like?
It blows at me
When I ride my bike.

It goes very fast
That is not fair
I really hate it
When it gets to my hair.

The wind, the wind,
Where does it go?
East, west, north, south?
I guess we'll never know.

Emma Wootton (9)
St Peter's RC Primary School, Bloxwich

Dolphins

Dolphin, dolphin jumping high,
High enough to reach the sky.
Doing somersaults in the air,
Making sure people know they are there.

People, people clapping and cheering,
Watching the dolphins as they are appearing.
Up and down, round and round,
Looking for things that need to be found.

Underwater dolphins swim,
Among the tropical fish.
As they start jumping high,
Up and down through the sky.

Dolphin, dolphin jumping high,
High enough to reach the sky.
Doing somersaults in the air,
Making sure people know they are there.

Natalie Brown (9)
St Peter's RC Primary School, Bloxwich

The Wind

The wind, the wind, it is mad,
It blows, it blows, it blows, so it's mad,
The wind blows, the wind blows, oh how so mad,
How mad can the wind blow? Just how mad?
The wind goes around the world so fast it goes,
It goes round the world, really mad,
So now you know how mad the wind is,
The wind, the wind, it is really mad.

Megan Hayward (8)
St Peter's RC Primary School, Bloxwich

Teachers

Teachers, I will never know,
How they just drone on all day,
How could they be quite that cruel,
And waste our lives away?

Why do they always disbelieve,
Each false excuse we say,
Like, 'Um, the dog ate it, Sir',
Or, 'My pet ant died today'?

And why do they always pick on,
Poor kids like you and me,
And keep us in from playtime,
When we simply must be free?

I will never quite understand,
No children ever will,
Why teachers from their planet come,
With textbooks set to kill?

Lydia Brookes (10)
St Peter's RC Primary School, Bloxwich

The Park

The park is colourful and bright,
The sun comes down giving light,
Children are full of joy,
Each girl and every boy,
What a beautiful sight,
People flying their kite,
The trees that flow and sway,
Twirls and rustles every day,
Children buying ice cream,
Flowers as beautiful as seen,
Lovely, long green grass,
That people like to pass.

Sophie Ebbans (8)
St Peter's RC Primary School, Bloxwich

The Snowman

Snowman, snowman
Made with care
Snowman, snowman
With no hair
Snowman, snowman
With a carrot nose
Snowman, snowman
No one knows
Snowman, snowman
With a black hat
Snowman, snowman
Lives with a little cat
Snowman, snowman
But then comes summer
Snowman, snowman
Vanishing away
Snowman, snowman
An old snowman has melted away.

Matthew Carter (9)
St Peter's RC Primary School, Bloxwich

Easter Bunnies

Easter bunnies cuddly and sweet,
When you see them, you'll agree they are a treat.
Some soft and white, some brown and furry,
Some will drive you topsy-turvy.

Cradle them in your arms,
Keep them safe from any harm.
Love them until the end,
For it's on you that they depend.

Make sure they know that you are there,
And that all you do for them is care.
Love and cherishment is all they need,
If that's what you're doing then you will succeed.

Hannah Jones & Eve Higginson (9)
St Peter's RC Primary School, Bloxwich

The Canticle Of Creation

My God, my Father, I honour Your love,
You brought me to the Earth by the spirit of Your dove,
You made the sun to cover darkness,
You made the moon and stars to shine over night,
You made the fire to warm me up,
You made the water to clean me up,
You made all creatures big and small,
You made me little but my mom and dad tall.

My Lord Jesus Christ comes down to show love,
You made peace in the world,
You made violence stoppable,
You helped all the people who were in need,
You shouted at people, who made violence for fun,
You sacrificed Yourself to save Your people,
And You made the world so every peaceful.

My Lord, Holy Spirit, You take good souls to Heaven,
You take bad souls to Hell,
You came from the one Father,
You helped Him to do what He has,
And that's what I like about You.

Sean Adams (9)
St Peter's RC Primary School, Bloxwich

Life Poem

When I was one I ate a bun,
When I was two I had a shoe.
When I was three I climbed a tree,
When I was four I climbed a door,
When I was five I had a beehive,
The day I went to sea it was just you and me.

Emily Stretton (8)
St Peter's RC Primary School, Bloxwich

My Life

When I was one
My first word was mom.
When I was two
I fell down the loo.
When I was three
I tried a cup of tea.
When I was four
I scratched the door.
When I was five
I got stuck on a beehive.
When I was six
I poked myself with a stick.
When I was seven
I went to Devon.
When I was eight
I had a best mate.
When I was nine
Everything was mine.
When I was ten
I was happy again!

Charlotte Essex (10)
St Peter's RC Primary School, Bloxwich

Christmas Eve

Here comes old Saint Nick
His sleigh is very quick,
You can hear the hooves
On everybody's roofs,
On the roof he will glide
Quieter than on a slide,
He fills stockings full of toys,
Some for girls, some for boys.

Alex Jones & Jack Bailey (9)
St Peter's RC Primary School, Bloxwich

The Titanic

Here the Titanic comes,
The biggest ship on the sea.
They say the ship is unsinkable,
And there's room for you and me.

We are now on the Atlantic Ocean,
Absolutely cold.
We saw the iceberg and started to scream,
And then the Titanic was foretold.

Not many people survived,
Only a few people were saved,
They were very lucky,
And to save themselves they waved.

Thomas Bannister (10)
St Peter's RC Primary School, Bloxwich

Bunny Rabbits

Bunny, bunny hopping
Around in the night
With the fire
Burning bright.

Bunny, bunny hopping
Around in the night
With the wind
Blowing out of sight.

Bunny, bunny hopping
Around in the night
With the snow
Falling clear and white.

Jessica Giusa & Stevie Ann Faulkner (10)
St Peter's RC Primary School, Bloxwich

Shark Attack

Shark, shark in the deep blue sea
I am scared it might attack me
The shark is deadly, the shark is cunning
Eyes watching us every day as we sit beside the bay
The fin signals the shark is coming
You can hear the sweetest birds coming
As the waves rock forward and back
It is time for the shark to attack
You can hear the people cry
With this shark they might die
Now we feel the wrath of the sea
We are not filled with glee
The shark is quick
The shark is quiet
Sharks eat so much they should go on a diet
Then there is the great white
That enjoys gliding through the sea at night
But not when it is light
The shark is great
The shark is big
I suggest it would be good at tig
The shark is not meek
It is time for it to go to sleep.

Brett Kelly (9)
St Peter's RC Primary School, Bloxwich

World

I had a dream when the world began,
That my dad was the moon and the sun was my mum.
All of the kids were the glittery stars,
And went to play on the planet Mars.
We cried and cried like little sheep,
The world was still silent and asleep.

Natasha Faraci (8)
St Peter's RC Primary School, Bloxwich

Christmas Joys!

Christmas is a joyful time,
It's when we sing carols and rhymes,
We dance around the Christmas tree,
And we all join in happily.

We hear the bells on Santa's sleigh,
To give presents to us today,
Rudolph with his shiny nose,
And Santa with his Christmas pose.

We hear the Christmas bells ringing,
And the carol singers singing,
We have some turkey for our dinner,
Those won't make us any thinner.

Christmas Day is nearly over,
We wish upon a four-leafed clover,
That next Christmas will be just as fun,
And we won't forget this one.

Abbie Gorman (11)
St Peter's RC Primary School, Bloxwich

My Parrot Alfie

Little Alfie in his cage,
He is only one year of age.
He is always squawking at his toys,
His babies are both boys.

He always pecks at his food,
So now Alfie will not be in a mood.
No one stands in his way,
But if they do they will have to pay.

When the day is over and he goes to bed,
He always has his goodnight kiss on his head.

Chelsea Khan (9)
St Peter's RC Primary School, Bloxwich

A Poem About My Life!

My family is going crazy,
My brother's like a baby,
My house is going mad,
My mom is turning really bad.

Me and dad are cool,
We've always hated school,
We both love friends,
My dad always mends.

I make a lot of things,
My mom wears some rings,
My dad likes cars,
And my brother, Mars bars.

My room is neat,
And my brother's is a junk street,
Me and my brother have a staff,
And he is called Taff.

I have lots of fun,
I have my fun in the sun,
So now you know about me,
Oh and I have a pear tree.

Charlotte Harper (10)
St Peter's RC Primary School, Bloxwich

The Sun

The sun shines brightly as bright as it will go.
I play in the garden with my little red bike.
Then I go back in and eat my tea,
And the sun is shining right on me.

Paige Cullum (8)
St Peter's RC Primary School, Bloxwich

When I Look . . .

When I look into the stars
I wonder if I can see Mars
I gaze and look
I look and gaze
But all of a sudden it becomes a big maze

I often look at the moon
And think of the cow and the spoon
I wonder if he has a face
Or if he's looking into space?

The brightest star of all
Is the soul of a loved one standing tall
I do hope that this is true
My nan and grandad won't feel so blue.

The open space, the black of the sky
A million souls out there just lie
A shooting star is a soul in a hurry
Or maybe the moon's got it all in a flurry.

Whatever is out there
We will never know
So peaceful, so calm, no stress and no harm
All the souls can rest in peace
And the time will travel just as it does week after week.

Chloe-Leigh Carr (10)
St Peter's RC Primary School, Bloxwich

Flowers

Flowers are the prettiest things I have ever seen,
People say they sparkle up the scene.

You can plant them in pots or by rocks,
Either way they are splendid things.

Chantelle Cassidy (11)
St Peter's RC Primary School, Bloxwich

School Dinners

Have you seen the school's custard?
It's all yellow and brown with blobs of mustard,
When we tried it at the school,
We all scrunched up and started to drool.

Have you seen the school's gravy?
To dispose of it we need the navy,
When we tried it at the school,
We were sick and sick in the pool.

Have you seen the school's chips?
They're red and pink and taste like lips,
When we tried them in the day,
We were sick and sick and so was Jay.

Have you seen the school's drink?
It's white, yellow and also pink,
We hold our nose to put it in,
Then we spit it in the bin.

So *don't* ever try school dinners!

Patricia Stych (10)
St Peter's RC Primary School, Bloxwich

Sky, Sky

The sky, the sky,
How I wish I could fly,
Up, up in the air,
I lie down and stare,
When I look at the sight,
I really want a flight,
The clouds are white,
They fade in the night.

Rhiannon Farrell (8)
St Peter's RC Primary School, Bloxwich

Cowboys

As mustangs charge around Stodge City
one mustang stands alone, but you should not have pity
this is Rumpo Kid's ride and always stands at his side
many gunslingers have died and lost their ride
the Rumpo Kid thinks he is the best in the west
that many of his enemies have been put to the test
there is a new lawman in town and he is wearing a frown
folk all think Sheriff Marshall P Knutt is a clown
sent in by the judge for he had a grudge
to free the town of the Rumpo Kid because he wouldn't budge
now Marshall P Knutt was a cowardly man
but needed to save the town however he can
with guns blazing he came out in the street
to show Rumpo that he'd be defeat
when his gun was empty Rumpo ran away
for the town, the Marshall had saved the day!

Zarozinia Wardle (11)
St Peter's RC Primary School, Bloxwich

Light And Dark

Light is very bright,
It keeps me safe at night.
Light is like a friend,
Because it never ends.
I don't like the dark,
Especially in the park.
It makes me very scared,
And it makes my hair stand on end.
Light and dark fills all the sky,
At different times but I don't know why.

Yasmine Foster (9)
St Peter's RC Primary School, Bloxwich

The Happy Poem

There was a dog
that met a frog
The dog was poorly
the frog was a doctor.
The frog put the
spoon in the dog's mouth
and made him have a rest.
The frog did a test
and played new tricks
the dog started to bark
he was all right now.

Aswaine Blake (9)
St Peter's RC Primary School, Bloxwich

The Sad Poem

There was a dog
That ate lots of frogs
He had a friend called Max
His owner paid lots of council tax
He ate a bowl of toxic waste
Soon he began to chew a lace
Then poor Max
Ate some ear wax
He stopped chasing cats
And sat on a mat
Now it's time for Max to die
So his friend said, 'Goodbye!'

Jamie O'Toole (9) & Riccardo
St Peter's RC Primary School, Bloxwich

Magic The Dragon

Magic the dragon lives in a dream
The most beautiful you have ever seen
Through magic lands she likes to fly
Look up and watch her, way up high.

Kiss me and cuddle me
Play with me and love me
I'll always be with you
And you'll be with me too.

Magic the dragon lives in a dream
The most beautiful you have ever seen
She'll fly away as far as you can see
You'll be her best friend
And so will she!

Melissa Parnaby (9)
The Croft School, Stratford-upon-Avon

The Classroom

If you went to the classroom,
You would get such a surprise!
People screaming everywhere,
Children telling lies.

You'd want to go away
To go somewhere else -
But no they've locked the door behind you,
So you squeak like a mouse!

Bill is standing on the table,
Chris is acting like a beast,
Jess is running around . . .
Well, they are children, at least!

Grace Rogers (10)
The Croft School, Stratford-upon-Avon

Playtime

P laytime is so much fun
L ooking for friends to play with
A ll of us play so well
Y ou and I have such good fun
T alking and playing
I t's always sad when playtime ends
M uch more fun tomorrow, but just now it's the
E nd of school.

Jessica Walley (9)
The Croft School, Stratford-upon-Avon

The Moon

The moon shimmers . . .
like a pearl on my mum's necklace
it glows like a highlighter nib on a desk
it sparkles like a diamond ring on my aunt's finger
it twinkles like a shot-put ball on the plastic rack
it shines like a dimmed light bulb inside my lamp
it floats like a lemon bath fizzer in the bath!

Kacie-Kimie Shanks (11)
The Croft School, Stratford-upon-Avon

Holiday

Everything packed
At the airport
Sunglasses on
Shorts and T-shirt
No plane!

Madeleine Hanrahan (10)
The Croft School, Stratford-upon-Avon

There Was A Young Mother Called Pam

There was a young mother called Pam
Who had a large cooking pan
When she was cooking
Her son went a-looking
For blueberry and strawberry jam.

Victoria Lougher (8)
The Croft School, Stratford-upon-Avon

Molly!

My fluffy doggy Molly is like a mini powder-puff!
She barks like a parrot, 'Woof, woof, woof.'

My little ball of fur would never give a purr
For she barks like a little puppy dog!

My sweet little Molly, I really love her so -
I wish she'd never leave, I wish she'd never go.

My puppy dog Molly, I would never give her up!
For she's my little puppy and that's just enough.

Chelsea Collindridge (11)
The Marsh Primary School, Blythe Bridge

Pencil Case

A pencil case is a coffin
With pencils stored away.
Locked so tight they cannot breathe
The rubbers are always scarred on corners.
Sharpeners are bloodstained
With thick sharpenings upon.
A ruler is a sword -
So straight it can rule and burn you.
All this out of a pencil case!

Brett Hopley (11)
The Marsh Primary School, Blythe Bridge

My Hamster

My hamster is like a black and white fluff ball,
A little bundle of love.
My hamster is a furry bath bomb,
A tiny racing car sprinting round his cage.
My hamster is like a minute torpedo shooting through water,
An evil-eyed, but cute fur ball.
My hamster is like a miniature velvety football,
A paper-eared freak.

Meg Jones (11)
The Marsh Primary School, Blythe Bridge

Teachers

Teachers are sly foxes
Crafty salesmen
Who give free samples of homework
Whilst acting as if they know all!
And as the pupils enter the classroom,
The teacher is there waiting
As the predator!
And we . . .
Are the prey!

Emilio Pinchi (11)
The Marsh Primary School, Blythe Bridge

Anger

Anger is like hot and fiery-red lava
Bubbling in your head.
Anger is like poison ivy
Touch it and you will come out in a rash.
Anger is like a nettle
Touch it and it will sting you.

Fran Maskery (11)
The Marsh Primary School, Blythe Bridge

Homework

It stalks me, it follows me,
It never goes away . . .
It's crimson, it's scarlet,
It's red lips too!

It's boring, it's evil,
It's an annoying rash.
It's garlic, it's chillies,
It's raw onions too!

It screams, it shouts,
It's a high-pitched woman.
It's a devil, it's a spot,
It's sunburn too!

It's maths, it's English,
It gets me every night!
It's science, it's history,
Every weekend too!

Argh - homework!

Francesca Lawton (11)
The Marsh Primary School, Blythe Bridge

Car

The engine is like a growling lion
The wipers are like an alarm
The steering wheel is the London Eye
The clutch is like a fire hose
The gear stick is a flag pole
The seats are like a bouncy castle.

Matthew Brain (11)
The Marsh Primary School, Blythe Bridge

My Bedroom

My bed is a mountain
I try to get to the top.
As soon as I get halfway up
I never want to stop.
My desk is a labyrinth
Everything gets lost.
I try to find my homework
I can't . . . but I must.
My wardrobe is a tiny room -
Everything gets squashed.
When my clothes get crumpled up
My mum gets really cross!
My bedroom is a happy place
I go there when I'm sad.
I sit in bed and call my mum and ask,
'Where is Dad?'

Karl Sturdy (11)
The Marsh Primary School, Blythe Bridge

Trees

Trees are disguised monsters,
Howling wolves.
They reach out their arms,
Grab the bird, then pull,
But when it turns to summer,
They hide themselves away
With a scent of flowers
And a feel of hay.
How they change so quickly is quite surprising!
And then it turns to winter again
And they quit hiding!

Jessie Bourne (10)
The Marsh Primary School, Blythe Bridge

Sophie (My Pony)

Sophie is a huge, cuddly teddy.
She is a fed up person doing homework!

Her hair is a wig -
A big black wig!

She has ears as if she is a spaniel,
Big and hairy!

Her feet are the size of a Shrek 2 pencil case,
Small and little.

Her tail is Rapunzel's hair,
Long and wavy.

Sophie is the best pony
Ever!

Amy Heath (11)
The Marsh Primary School, Blythe Bridge

My Racquet

My racquet flings me round the court!
Up, down, left, right!
I have no control over it
Even though it's my favourite sport!
I fight to keep my score off nought
When we're playing, it talks and talks
It never shuts up!
'You have to run faster, you have to try harder!'
But when we're not playing, it's as quiet as a mouse.
So I lock it up tight,
When I get back to the house!

Becky Lunt (11)
The Marsh Primary School, Blythe Bridge

Homework

Homework caught me up last night,
Don't know how, but it gave me a fright,
'English, maths, history!'
These words it chanted, facing me.

'You lazy child, me you have found,
I eat small children: my belly's round,
You should have started at half-past three,
But of course you didn't, for you see me.'

'You silly girl! I'll gobble you up,
Spit your bones into a plastic cup,
So now you know, you have been told,
Do our homework if you want to grow old.'

Charlotte Leigh Nixon (11)
The Marsh Primary School, Blythe Bridge

Harry My Cat

Harry is a torpedo
When he zooms everywhere!

He is Spider-Man
When he climbs up everything!

He is a mean, lean, licking machine
In the morning!

He is a one inch animal
Because he can fit through anything!

He miaows often because
He has nobody to play with!

Alex Davies (11)
The Marsh Primary School, Blythe Bridge

My Brother Jake

Jake is like a cute, cuddly toy
You can hug all day.
He's like a lion
Roaring in your face.
Jake smells like
An impeccable, posh boy.
He's like a meanie on the outside,
But inside he's a big softy!
Jake is like a three-eyed monster!

Josh Forrester (10)
The Marsh Primary School, Blythe Bridge

Rosie The Retriever

Rosie the retriever is like a cuddly toy
Her barks sound like an elephant's stomp!
When she has been washed
She smells like a vanilla-scented candle.
I think she looks like a dog-shaped snowman
And when I go home to her after school
She acts like a hyper hyena!

Andrew Cresswell (11)
The Marsh Primary School, Blythe Bridge

Friendship

Friendship is the colour of lemon-yellow,
It smells like flowers and coloured sweets,
It tastes like fresh, pure apple juice,
It sounds like birds singing in the trees, and
It feels like joy inside you and children laughing,
Friendship lives in the heart.

Jodie Moss (10)
The Marsh Primary School, Blythe Bridge

Friendship

Friendship is orange,
It smells like a big bar of milk chocolate,
Friendship tastes sweet and wonderful,
It sounds like a mermaid singing,
It feels like a soft teddy bear,
Friendship lives in your heart forever.

Hollie Archibald (10)
The Marsh Primary School, Blythe Bridge

Friendship

Is the colour of lilac
It tastes like caramel chocolate
It sounds like happy people laughing
It feels like playing cheerfully
It lives in your heart.

Rachel Davis (9)
The Marsh Primary School, Blythe Bridge

War

War is the colour of khaki
It smells like dead people
It tastes like blood
It feels like I am going to die
It lives in a battlefield
It sounds like a bullet banging.

George Scott (10)
The Marsh Primary School, Blythe Bridge

Misery

Misery is a dark blue
It smells like burning oil
Misery tastes like mouldy teacakes
It sounds like crying
It feels like cruelty
It lives in a dark, gloomy cave.

George Podmore (9)
The Marsh Primary School, Blythe Bridge

My Dog Beryl

My dog is like a cute bundle of love
When she barks it's like . . .
A big horn being pressed in your ear
She smells like a sloppy fish
She feels like a bundle of candyfloss
When she's active she's like a chilli-filled chinchilla
I think she looks like a dog-shaped panda
But I love her and I am proud to have her!

Jack Bailey (11)
The Marsh Primary School, Blythe Bridge

Flowers

Flowers are like pieces of cotton wool,
Other flowers are like bells,
Others are so squashed together they are like carpets,
Some are so spread out they are like unhappy planets.

Aaron Walker (10)
The Marsh Primary School, Blythe Bridge

Frustration

Dark scarlet is the colour of frustration
It smells like poison
It tastes chewy and never-ending
It sounds like sharp nails scratching a blackboard
It feels like sharp pieces of glass sticking in you
It lives in the smallest jail in the world.

Jack Lane (10)
The Marsh Primary School, Blythe Bridge

Hope

Hope is blue
It smells like violets swaying in the breeze
It tastes like white chocolate
Hope sounds like a cat purring
It feels like wool
Hope lives in the most unlikely places.

Thomas Johnson (9)
The Marsh Primary School, Blythe Bridge

Peace

Peace is the colour of sky-blue
It smells like a bunch of red roses
Peace tastes like orange jelly
It sounds like birds sweetly singing
Peace feels like soft warm fur
Peace lives in your heart!

Isobel Rowley (9)
The Marsh Primary School, Blythe Bridge

Death

Death
A horrible monster
A bad-tempered Darth Vader
When it strikes, it hurts
Like someone's slit your throat
The bitter apple taste
Burning your mouth
Lurking . . .
Where nobody goes
You're dying as well
The mystery of darkness
Swerving
Around you like a snake
Clawing
Like a tiger
Then it floats
Away
Whispering,
'Come with me,
Come with me.'

Amy Leese (10)
The Marsh Primary School, Blythe Bridge

War

War is the colour of grey
It smells like smoke from a gun
War tastes burnt and bitter
It sounds like screams and bangs
It feels like pain
War lives in the heart of soldiers.

Megan Rowley (9)
The Marsh Primary School, Blythe Bridge

Homework

Homework can talk
But never see
It's hideous!

I'm accused of being lazy
The homework says I'm crazy
It's hideous!

The teacher gave it
She should do it
It's hideous!

It bit me so I ripped it up
I'm in Heaven
Homework's history, hideous!

I went in the metal graveyard
For a funeral
The grave will return . . .
By coming back to life!

Emily Mason (11)
The Marsh Primary School, Blythe Bridge

Love

Love is the colour of pink
It smells like sweet strawberries
It tastes like creamy-white chocolate
It sounds like a romantic song
It feels like a cuddly teddy
It lives in people's hearts.

Charlie Alderson (10)
The Marsh Primary School, Blythe Bridge

My Sister Sam

Sam is a robot monster
An alien from outer space!
I notice her strange behaviour,
With war paint all over her face!
I think she calls it make-up, but . . .
I'm not completely sure
Her planet's not like ET
They keep coming back for more!
She despises outdoors
And she despises cheese
Every time you see her face
You're gonna heave!
So now I leave you with one
Almighty warning . . .
Her kind could be anywhere
In your bedroom or your . . .
Awning!

Liz Bailes (11)
The Marsh Primary School, Blythe Bridge

The Magic Box

(Based on 'Magic Box' by Kit Wright)

I will put in the box . . .
A furry cat with a magic tail
A gold pearl on a boat
A dragon with no fire!

I will put in the box . . .
A magic piece of silk
That turns people into dust.

My box is made of a very old skull
It has an eyeball as a lock
A bone as a key.

I will go in my box
To a lava pond to find treasure.

Shawn Peach (10)
Uffculme Special School, Moseley

The Magic Box

(Based on 'Magic Box' by Kit Wright)

I will put in the box . . .
A sandy seaside with a red-hot sun
And a big silver shark in the sea
And I would see the world on a boat.

I will put in the box . . .
A big, yellow mat that could fly
And a big, fat, lazy cat
That could take me round the world
That talks English.

My box is made from . . .
A dragon's skin and gold
The skin is red and green
That shines in the sun.

I will go in my box to . . .
The Second World War
And help people everywhere
And then go home
To my magical bed.

Jake Duggins (11)
Uffculme Special School, Moseley

The Magic Box

(Based on 'Magic Box' by Kit Wright)

I will put in the box . . .
A heart
A jewellery box with earrings.

I will put in the box . . .
A cute kitten with a soft tail.

I will put in the box . . .
A picture of me for Mrs Castrell.

Laura Roberts (11)
Uffculme Special School, Moseley

The Magic Box

(Based on 'Magic Box' by Kit Wright)

I will put in the box . . .
A mirror to see into the future
It takes you there.

I will put in the box . . .
A belching dinosaur that belches every minute
With a big, bulging belly.

My box is made from . . .
Dragons' teeth and gold
And magic and silver bars and phoenix fire.

I will go in my box to . . .
The land of magical creatures with an old phoenix
And search for things that you have never heard of!

Marcus Garnham (10)
Uffculme Special School, Moseley

The Magic Box

(Based on 'Magic Box' by Kit Wright)

I will put in the box . . .
A magic key that can take me anywhere
And it is made from human skin.

I will put in the box . . .
A monster that has big red eyes
That is heat sensored so he can track down food.

My box is made from gold
And it has shining red corners and dark secrets.

I will go in my box to the sea
To see some rainbow fish and the dark ocean.

Jack Milton (10)
Uffculme Special School, Moseley

The Magic Box

(Based on 'Magic Box' by Kit Wright)

I will put in the box . . .
A magic book that can take me to the past
A magic pin that can turn into a man.

I will put in the box . . .
A fluffy puppy dog
A holiday and a happy man that tells jokes
An old radio that plays strange music.

My box is made from gold, rock and wax
It has some magic mud and has money inside it.

I will go in my box to Ibiza
Where I will play on the beach.

Ian Wager (10)
Uffculme Special School, Moseley

The Magic Box

(Based on 'Magic Box' by Kit Wright)

I will put in the box . . .
A big, shiny dragon that is breathing fire.

I will put in the box . . .
A big battleship of solid gold.

I will put in the box . . .
A magic spell that glimmers and gives me what I want.

Jeavan Garcha (10)
Uffculme Special School, Moseley

The Magic Box

(Based on 'Magic Box' by Kit Wright)

I will put in the box . . .
A pretty doll wearing a pink dress.

I will put in the box . . .
A heart-shaped music box that is beautiful.

I will put in the box . . .
A fat cat that is yellow, nice and cute.

Chloe Jinks (10)
Uffculme Special School, Moseley

Winter Poem

I stare at the tree outside,
A robin jumps on its branch
Which covers the robin from view,
And when the bird appears again,
Its song for help, has been silenced.

The snowflakes gently fall
And start to gnaw the ground,
Until only they remain
And as the blizzard continues to fire,
Snow has conquered the war.

Children try to make snowmen,
But the blizzard drives them in.
Clouds turn evil and black
The icicles harden their hard armour
And begin the march of winter.

Then the icicles halt,
The sun glows and defeats them all.
Buds begin to grow into flowers
And overpowers the snow.
The robin sings again.

James Bateman (10)
Wood Green Junior School, Wednesbury

Winter Poem

Branches of trees glisten and drip,
Silvery snowflakes dance in the air.
Delicate wind twirls selfish and sour
As the twigs of trees turn cold and bare.

Winter stretches out her long, harsh hands
And entombs the world in her grip,
As a little red robin sings, cold and sweet,
When the spirits of ice gnaw and rip.

A soft mound of snow is winter's bed,
A soft winter breeze is her curtain pale,
Shimmering blue icicles are her xylophone,
Woven cobwebs her window veil.

Her icy eyes burn freezing blue
As the wave of spring brings fresh and new.

Eleanor Ashfield-Hayes (11)
Wood Green Junior School, Wednesbury

I Wanna Be A Millionaire!

(Inspired by 'I Wanna Be A Superstar' by Charles Thomson)

I wanna be a millionaire!
I wanna have pink funky hair,
I wanna go and live in Spain.
I wanna own a private plane,
I wanna have a limousine.
I wanna boyfriend who's name is Dean,
I wanna spend without a care,
I wanna be a millionaire!
I wanna shopping spree in France,
I wanna jump, sing and dance.
I wanna own a mansion too,
I wanna paint the kitchen blue.
I wanna be a famous model,
I wanna penguin that can waddle,
I wanna be a millionaire.

Robyn Lea (10)
Woodlands School, Willenhall

Rhyming Couplets

(Inspired by 'I Wanna Be A Superstar' by Charles Thomson)

I wanna be a *dancing queen,*
I wanna drive a limousine,
I wanna be in pantomimes,
I wanna have lots of lines.
I wanna holiday that's really sunny,
I wanna be a *dancing queen,*
I wanna dance and sing, not be mean.
I wanna travel all over the world,
I wanna have my hair all curled.
I wanna have a massive house,
I wanna own a tiny mouse.
I wanna be a *dancing queen.*

Rebecca Jones (10)
Woodlands School, Willenhall

In The Street

Up there, down the street,
That's where all us kids meet,
Blazing with red-hot heat.
Whilst we are sitting in the shade,
While we shout for my maid,
Then we start to sing, following the beat.

Shannon Guy (11)
Woodlands School, Willenhall

Little Blue Riding Hood

One day Little Blue Riding Hood
Was in the park as she should
To a bird she started talking
And slowly walking
She got covered in lots of mud.

Rachael Powers (10)
Woodlands School, Willenhall

Limerick

Do you know how hard and deadly slick
It is to write a limerick?
The lines are so hard to do
I flushed the first lot down the loo.

Secondly they have to grow
With all the words I need to know
That's why I'll tell you now
While wiping the sweat off my brow
For everybody, plain to see
It's the hardest form of poetry!

Aaron Green (11)
Woodlands School, Willenhall

Sunset (Cinquain)

Red clouds,
Traffic dies down,
Sun on the horizon,
A time of calm tranquillity,
Sunset.

Adam Holland (10)
Woodlands School, Willenhall

Cinquain

Springtime,
River flowing,
Sun shining all day long,
Darkness comes with bright stars shining,
Springtime.

Laura Stanley (11)
Woodlands School, Willenhall

A Wanna Be A Movie Star

(Inspired by 'I Wanna Be A Superstar' by Charles Thomson)

I wanna be a movie star
I wanna drive a silver sports car
I wanna boat and own my own plane
I wanna horse with a long flowing mane
I wanna watch made of gold
I wanna never ever grow old
I wanna have my own wooden bar
I wanna be a movie star
I wanna dress all in white
I wanna have a chocolate bath
I wanna have friends that make me laugh
I wanna be a disco queen
I wanna have a limousine
I wanna fly a sparkly kite
I wanna be a movie star.

Faye Haddon (10)
Woodlands School, Willenhall

Crazy Star

(Inspired by 'I Wanna Be A Superstar' by Charles Thomson)

I wanna be a crazy star
I wanna drive a silver car
I wanna shake my hair all loose
I wanna bring back chocolate mousse
I wanna wear crazy clothes
I wanna wear bright red bows
I wanna drive so, so far
I wanna be a crazy star
I wanna call my rabbit 'Par'
I wanna go on a massive cruise
I wanna drink lots of booze
I wanna flash my blue suede shoes
I wanna have my own private loos
I wanna fly to planet Mars
I wanna be a crazy star.

Farrah Turbin (10)
Woodlands School, Willenhall

Lord Of The Rings

Lord of the Rings isn't very funny,
But Gimli the dwarf has a very big tummy.
Aragorn always wins the fight!
Gandalf turned from grey to white.

Fighting Orcs and Uruk-hai too,
Never stopping for the loo!
Saruman making Orcs underground,
Never ever to be found.

Sauron's big fiery eye,
On a tower, very high!
Legolas arrows all the Orcs,
Aragorn kills more and more.

Treebeard the Ent is very tall,
The hobbits are clever but very small.
Their friend Gollum is very lonely,
He lives in a cave which isn't very homely.

Frodo and Sam are going to Mount Doom,
I hope they get there very soon.
As the Fellowship fight, more and more,
Frodo and Sam get to the mountain's core.

Ross Whitehouse & Jordan Speed (10)
Woodlands School, Willenhall

Untitled

I'm your beginning and end
I'm always at your side
And I'm your twin friend
I'm never in colour
Except black.
What am I?

James Moore (10)
Woodlands School, Willenhall

I Want To Be A Spoilt Brat!

(Inspired by 'I Wanna Be A Superstar' by Charles Thomson)

I want to be a spoilt brat!
I want to own a killer cat.
I want to swim in a chocolate sea,
I want to own the city's key.
I want to rule every living thing,
Then I'll want to be a king!
I want to be a spoilt brat!
I want to own a magic wand,
Then I'll turn my hair light blond.
I want a hamster, green and red,
I'll let him share my double bed.
Then I'll buy a fluffy dog,
Feed him to my smelly frog.
I want to have a giant rat,
That's why I'll be a spoilt brat!

Zac Thomson (11)
Woodlands School, Willenhall

I Wanna Be A Film Star!

(Inspired by 'I Wanna Be A Superstar' by Charles Thomson)

I wanna be a film star!
I wanna have my name splashed on every car.
I wanna be on everyone's TV
I don't wanna be caught on CCTV.
I wanna play the main part,
I wanna be driven around in a cart.
I wanna be a film star!
I wanna be in every film that is made,
I never wanna fade.
I wanna own my own private jet,
I don't wanna ever be in debt!
I wanna own my own flash drum kit,
I never wanna have an electric fit.
I wanna be a film star!

Danielle Amy Vernon (10)
Woodlands School, Willenhall

I Wanna Be A Millionaire!

(Inspired by 'I Wanna Be A Superstar' by Charles Thomson)

I wanna be a millionaire!
I wanna do things without a care
I wanna own a massive home
I wanna have a swimming pool dome
I wanna own a limousine
I wanna be in a magazine
I wanna fly right through the air
I wanna be a millionaire!
I wanna live in Australia
I wanna surf like mania
I wanna own a chocolate land
I wanna be in my own band
I wanna chill out every day
I wanna go on holiday in May
I wanna have people stop and stare
I wanna be a millionaire!

Natalie Carless & Charlotte Sanders (11)
Woodlands School, Willenhall

A Riddle

A lot of keys
A mouse running round
A screen any colour,
And any sound.
All connected
Down loading,
Disk holding.

Can you guess?

Liam Kirk (11)
Woodlands School, Willenhall